MW00659260

The Modern Seller
Copyright © 2018 by Amy Franko

All rights are reserved.

No part of this publication may be reproduced, distributed or transmitted in any form or by any means, including photocopying, recording or other digital or mechanical methods, without the prior written permission of the author, except in the cases of fair use as permitted by U.S. and international copyright laws. For permission requests, please submit in writing to the publisher at the address below:

Published by:
Smart Business Network
835 Sharon Drive, Suite 200
Westlake, OH 44145

Printed in the United States of America
Editor: Dustin S. Klein

ISBN: 978-1-945389-62-7
Library of Congress Control Number: 2018943075

Printed in USA

THE **MODERN** SELLER

SELL MORE AND
INCREASE YOUR IMPACT
IN THE NEW SALES ECONOMY

BY **AMY FRANKO**

SMART BUSINESS® BOOKS
An Imprint of Smart Business® Network Inc.

TABLE OF CONTENTS

AUTHOR'S NOTE

When I began my career in sales, I was fortunate to work for one of the most recognizable names in the world, IBM, and then later, Lenovo. I'm forever grateful for that opportunity; it has opened more doors and created more value in my life than I ever could've imagined. It was the power of my network that created an opportunity to get into the field, one that really wasn't even on my radar (more on that in the book). I know I wouldn't be here in this moment, with a published book, if it weren't for my IBM experience.

There were a couple of defining moments while at IBM that made me realize I was in the right place. One was that my first, second, and third-line sales leaders were all women, which even today is probably still a unique experience. This trifecta of awesome women leaders were my role models; I could see myself in them, and I could picture myself being successful in my role.

The other moment was being mentored early on by two of the most successful sales professionals that I know. Their creativity and drive, the way they worked with customers, and the ownership they took for their success were all things I learned to emulate. Those mentors helped me as I shaped my identity in sales.

Sales is absolutely the best field I could've "fallen" into in my life. I didn't intentionally choose to get into sales, I think it chose me. I can't think of any other profession where I can direct my destiny, stretch myself, and create my own success.

Probably like your career path, mine has taken winding roads. Most of us will have up to seven distinct careers in our lifetimes. I'm talking seven entirely different fields without much crossover. I've been in at least four different industries with distinct roles in information technology, sales, training, and now as an entrepreneur with a consulting business.

In looking back through all those transitions, selling is the skill I can point to that has had the biggest impact. Whereas early in my career I saw the profession more as a path to create my own success, I now realize it also taught me I could use it to create more impact for others. It gave me the courage to step into entrepreneurship, because I knew I had what it took to build a client base. It helps me to build better relationships, to create bigger opportunities for myself and those around me, and to help others succeed. All those things encompass what makes the selling profession so rewarding.

Ever since I can remember, I knew there were three things I wanted to do: create, lead, and write. I've had lots of opportunities to do all three, but "writing the damn book" was the one thing that continued to sit on the list. It was a longtime goal in need of a jumpstart. Then my good friend and fellow entrepreneur JJ DiGeronimo introduced me to Dustin S. Klein at Smart Business Books. That got me into gear to take the first step. The first step led to the next, and then the next. Writing this book became a reality, one page at a time.

Who is this book for?

Here's who I envisioned as I wrote this book. I've worn nearly all these hats. For those I haven't worn, I've worked alongside you or for you at some point in my career:

- **Sales professionals,** who want better strategies to win new business and maintain high-value clients
- **Sales leaders,** who want "A" teams, and to be the leader that every "A" player wants to work for
- **Learning professionals,** who want to establish or maintain a seat at the business table; they need to make sure that sales training programs align to what sales organizations need today
- **Sales enablement professionals,** who are the glue between sales, training, and marketing; they want to make sure that sales enablement strategies and tools are aligned to sales

There are so many sales books out there. One of the challenges I write about is that we're living in a world of sameness. For any given need there are so many choices out there, and they often look alike.

So, why is this book worth your time?
Your success as a sales professional or sales leader depends on building the skills I lay out in the book. This isn't a book on skills like prospecting, presenting, negotiating, or closing. There are lots of terrific books out there on those topics, and the need for these foundational skills will never go away. It's necessary now to pair them with what I call the "skills behind the skills." They're the skills that will make you better at the tactical aspects of selling, and direct you more strategically.

Your role could look drastically different in just a few years' time, and you need to be ready. The pace of change is relentless in this age of digital transformation. Your company may look very different in five years, or may not exist at all in its current form. Companies that exist only in an entrepreneur's dream today may be your biggest competitor tomorrow. Disruption is everywhere, and you have a choice. If you choose to lead yourself and others through it, this book is for you.

As of this writing in late 2017, I'm returning from the Sales 3.0 Conference hosted by *Selling Power* and Gerhard Gschwandtner. Some bold predictions came out of that conference. Even if a fraction of this comes true, it's still big change for you:

a) Fifty percent of leading companies will not be here in 10 years.
b) All companies will be 100 percent digital by 2020.
c) Three million sales jobs will be gone in five years, which will create a survival imperative. There will need to be a 200 percent increase in sales productivity per sales professional, and sales staff will decrease by 20 percent in five years.

If your CEO is challenging you to grow into new markets, expand existing markets, or open an entirely new category of products and services, then you need an exponential mindset. This is a concept I was first introduced to by Mark Bonchek of Shift Thinking. Most of us are conditioned to think incrementally; we're focused on what's right in front of us. This linear thought pattern is useful for steady growth, but it's also limited to the goals we can easily see. Daily sales activities are often incremental. An exponential mindset is what Mark refers to as "10X growth." It gets us thinking differently—about the value we create, how we can be different, and accomplishing the big goals we can't even see yet. The skills in this book are exponential skills, and when paired with incremental skills, can get you that 10X: 10X engagement, 10X productivity, 10X value.

How is the book organized?

The New Sales Economy. This section is about what our decision makers are facing in today's business environments. Sure, some of the usual ones made the list, like technology and information overload. But they're talked about so often, they're almost cliché. I dig into some others I've uncovered in interviews, research, and from my own experiences. They'll make you think differently about what needs to be on your radar.

Make Way for the Modern Seller. I share a bit about my own "light bulb" moment that began my modern seller journey. It's not an overnight transition, that's for sure—and I'm still evolving as the profession evolves. I also introduce a working definition for the modern seller, which sets up the rest of our conversation in the book. Lastly, I introduce the Five Dimensions of the Modern Seller, which contribute to creating sellers, leaders, and sales organizations that will succeed in the new sales economy. They are:

- Agile
- Entrepreneurial
- Holistic

- Social
- Ambassador

Five Dimensions of the Modern Seller. This is where we get into specifics on each one. The book is designed to be modular; so you can begin with the dimension matters most to you right now and jump to others in any order that works best for you.

The book is also designed to be practical. While I do reference research, I'm focused on how you can apply the concepts in selling situations, or how you can incorporate them into your sales strategies and training programs. For every modern selling dimension, you'll learn:

- ***Why it matters*** to sales results and business growth
- ***What the skillset looks like in action,*** in everyday selling situations
- ***Specific behaviors*** to cultivate within each dimension
- ***Specific actions*** you can apply as a modern seller and a modern sales leader

For learning and development or sales enablement professionals, these skills and behaviors can be integrated into your competency models, strategies, and learning programs that support the sales organization.

I look forward to sharing this journey with you, as we all continue to evolve as modern sellers and leaders. This is a book about leadership as much as it's a book about sales. In the end, it's about our leadership—no matter our title. We all have the choice and the capacity to be role models, to influence, and to impact the greater good. A choice to lead. I hope this book gives you the tools to do just that.

Amy Franko
June 2018

INTRODUCTION

The New Sales Economy—So, what's changed?

My client was in the midst of a huge technology transformation, a multi-year initiative that would completely change the way this company did business with its customers. This was one of those no-fail initiatives, and every role in the billion-dollar organization would be touched. Everyone would be dealing with this change and how it affected them, plus helping their customers to successfully navigate the changes.

After a lengthy RFP process, my firm was selected to design and develop the training that every team would need for a successful go live. As with any major technology initiative, we were building the plane as we were flying it. Systems were still undergoing development and testing, business rules and procedures were in a daily flux, and project priorities changed on a dime.

Now meet my decision maker.

It was 12 months earlier when the company brought in a new leader to build an employee learning organization. She was tasked with all organizational learning and development, plus making sure that every employee was trained and ready for go live. She was also hiring a new team and getting that team up to speed.

Because she's a strong leader, she quickly inherited another team. Shortly after that, another team. In the six months she had been there her team quadrupled to cover three major business support areas in addition to training. The workload quadrupled too—all business as usual, along with supporting this major technology initiative.

Because my decision maker now had this expanded role, she had a seat at the table with key executives, making sometimes weekly presentations. She was leading her expanded team and coaching them to be successful. She was also part of a cross-functional leadership team on organizational learning, and she played a key role in developing hundreds of people in her organization. Oh, and organizational changes were coming too, which meant people in their roles may be shifted, or even downsized.

She's constantly juggling these balls in the air, and almost every time slot of the day is double-booked with a meeting or phone call. There's barely time to breathe, let alone get a restroom break or eat lunch. What little open time she has is extremely valuable, to be protected at all costs. And she does it all with the most positive of attitudes and a smile on her face.

I remember one week when I suggested a strategy session to discuss some new ideas I had been researching. Her eyes lit up at the idea of getting offsite, investing time in just thinking about future priorities and where she'd like to head. But each date we looked at was tougher to schedule than the last, until it got to the point where we were looking at least three months out, when things "let up a bit." Too many urgent meetings, too many fires to be put out. No time, it would just have to wait.

The crazy thing about all these seemingly chaotic circumstances is that we're actually doing business together today, and she considers me a strategic partner! It's not easy to squeeze time into the calendar, even when you're "in" and have a trusted advisor status. Now imagine if this was a prospective customer who had yet to commit to an opportunity to work together. What would it take in that scenario to get one of those double-booked calendar slots? For our overloaded customers and prospects, it's a challenge just to bring forth new ideas and new ways of doing things, let alone creating meaningful change.

Welcome to the new sales economy—the intersection of business, technology, and cultural dynamics, all affecting the ways our prospects and clients interact with and buy from us. Anyone in a role that touches sales has to adapt if you're going to succeed—this means new mindsets, skillsets, and tools.

What makes it so tough in our decision makers' worlds?

Put yourself in the shoes of that decision maker. What's a typical day or week (if there is such a thing)? If your decision makers are like mine, they're challenged with running daily operations, without a sliver of extra time to think about how things could be different if they engaged with you. The easiest answer is often to make no change, especially when it's a struggle to keep it all moving under the existing structure.

Here are just a few things that affect their engagement with you. Some of these reasons are so ubiquitous that we've become immune to them. While these challenges can seem like insurmountable barriers to building relationships with our decision makers, they are also opportunities for the modern seller.

The need to differentiate with customers. In just about any industry you can imagine, buyers have become savvier, and their expectations of products and services only get more sophisticated. That creates a pace of change around product and service creation that's only going to accelerate. Our customers are asking themselves: "What do we need to do to remain competitive? How do we know that what we're bringing to market today will still be attractive to customers tomorrow? How can we be proactive and stay ahead of our competitors?"

Our customers are looking for their differentiation, that ability to stay a few steps ahead.

Technology. It's changing the way our customers operate both internally and with their customers. I have one client with three major technology transformations happening simultaneously—a new customer platform, a new enterprise email system and a new knowledge management platform. Technology transformations are often necessary; they're also multi-year and fatigue-inducing, zapping time, energy, and resources.

Constantly shifting priorities. Even the most surefire strategic priorities can change on a dime. What was completely top of mind today may fall to the bottom of the list tomorrow. This means our customers are reallocating their resources—these may be people resources, budget resources, time resources. This can create chaos, and it leaves our decision makers with fires to put out—taking away even more of their time to solve their key challenges or focus on growth.

Information overload and instant responses. I was giving a keynote for a client a few years ago and we met for dinner the evening before. When I got to the restaurant, she had her head buried in her phone, frantically typing with her thumbs and looking completely stressed. Even when she put the phone away, it was obvious throughout dinner that she was still lost in thought. She shared that she had over 200 emails in her inbox and was dreading the workload that waited for her once she got back to her hotel.

In 2014, business users sent and received an average of 121 emails per day, and by the end of 2018, that number is expected to grow to 140 emails per day. (http://www.radicati.com/wp/wp-content/uploads/2014/01/Email-Statistics-Report-2014-2018-Executive-Summary.pdf) This doesn't include texting or managing a growing number of social media accounts. While not every email requires a response, and some may not get one, it still takes up precious mental real estate. My instinct is to respond right away, to get it off my plate, and I've had to retrain myself. And that sense of dread you get when you know you have dozens of emails to reply to? That's not imaginary either—we're conditioned to reply quickly and dig ourselves out from information overload. In fact, more than 50 percent of email responses come within an hour, conditioning us to never be far from our inboxes. (https://www.forbes.com/sites/amymorin/2015/11/28/waiting-for-a-reply-study-explains-the-psychology-behind-email-response-time/#6347171b9755)

Change fatigue. It's tough to build relationships when your contact points are constantly changing, and that was the case with an enterprise account where I was developing new business. Every time I made some progress with a potential decision maker or influencer, within six months their role would change and they'd be reorganized into another area of the business. It happened so often, the organization became known for it. While it was frustrating for me, it was downright exhausting for those living with that every quarter.

It's so common, there's a name for it: organizational change fatigue. And, it goes against everything we as humans crave. We crave security, stability, and predictability. When we live with a heightened sense of stress over unanswered messages or unfinished tasks, it affects our ability to think clearly and engage. With organizational change initiatives failing at a rate of 70 percent, it's easy to see why we lose trust. We know the change won't stick, we become jaded, and we learn to live in this state of heightened alert. If I'm your decision maker, I'm likely going to avoid further upsetting the balance by introducing even more change. And who knows, I may not be your decision maker in six months because I've been moved into another role.

It's tough to find talent, and great talent often doesn't stay long. I remember when I made my very first hire. As an entrepreneur, I hit the employee lottery. Sarah was a rock star. She was hard working, ethical, creative, and engaged; she was all in on making the organization a success. I remember thinking how easy this was, why did everyone think that hiring was so hard? I fell into the trap of thinking I was great at hiring people.

Well, was I ever humbled. Fast forward about five years and four sales professionals later. I had failed miserably at finding and keeping sales talent, for a variety of reasons—some of it organizational and some of it individual. I learned that it's extremely tough to find the exact right hiring match. Replacing talent is expensive, and great talent doesn't often stay long. According to the U.S. Bureau of Labor Statistics, most of us will have up to seven distinct careers in our lifetime, and the average U.S. worker in a management or professional occupation will stay in that role for an average of 5.1 years. Your decision maker is likely in a continual talent search, or changing roles themselves.

Mergers and acquisitions. According to Gallup, acquisition is the current growth strategy of most *Forbes* Global 2000 companies.

I was part of an acquisition, my company was bought by a foreign organization with no track record in the U.S. It was almost as if our identities changed overnight, and that created a sense of chaos and uncertainty. While I only have my experience to validate it, productivity stalled for those first few weeks and months while we adjusted to a new normal. It stalled again for weeks and months after the transition. Some customers held off on major technology purchases until everything with the acquisition shook out. My teammates were deciding on whether to wait out the change or find other opportunities, and people were worried about whether they would have a role in the new organization.

When our decision makers are dealing with the effects of mergers or potential fallout from an acquisition, it takes away from their ability to think about strategic direction and growth.

Tumultuous is the new normal. Tune into any news outlet or social media, and something is always in a state of uncertainty.

These outside situations can have significant effect on our moods. Our moods, in turn, affect our decision making and judgments. The interesting part is that situations don't even necessarily have to be related to share the effects. This is known as incidental emotion, and can carry over from one situation to the next. This has real effects on our decision makers, both at a micro level (personal) and a macro level (organizational).

At a micro level, let's say your daily habit is listening to the news on your way into work. These days, almost every story is negative. If that negativity creates emotions of anger and fear, those emotions can stay with you. Without you even being aware, they can flow over into the next situation and affect its outcome, say a conversation with your spouse, a colleague, or that big meeting on your calendar this afternoon. So, if I'm your decision maker, my interaction with you could be affected by incidental emotion and may change what happens next.

Similarly, at a macro level, continuous uncertainty can cause organizations to be risk averse, shift strategy, or delay decisions, especially in complex situations. Outside uncertainty can create internal uncertainty. If I'm your decision maker, I may be calling to tell you that the project we're working on? It's delayed until after [fill in the blank] event has passed and the situation can be reassessed. Or it's now in front of a review committee, because multiple others will need to weigh in before a decision is made. This group think is increasingly common—it spreads out the decision-making risk, but it can also slow down decisions and progress toward a strategic goal.

Everything is important. Ask anyone how they're doing, and these days the answer is usually, "crazy busy." Or "Busy, but it's all good. I'm working on a million great things right now." We live in a world where everything is important, and it becomes harder and harder to cut through the clutter. When there are so many things to decide, and so many possible combinations to decide from, it becomes tough to differentiate one from the next. It's tough to see what's truly important versus what's trivial pretending to be important.

For our decision makers, when every priority and every task get equal weighting, their decisional playing field is leveled. What they thought was a problem yesterday has now been replaced with something else of equal importance. When nothing stays above the level, it's easy to fall back to the familiar status quo. That may mean staying with a current provider, or simply doing nothing to solve a current problem because something else now has their attention.

It's a world of sameness. I've been looking for a new CRM, and nearly every solution has similar features, benefits, and pricing structures. In short, they all look the same to me. They could all work. And because they all look the same to me and they could all work, guess what? I still haven't decided on which CRM is the best fit. I've delayed that decision because in a world of sameness, those decisions get crowded out by other things.

When our decision makers see sameness, they'll defer almost every time, especially if there aren't major negative consequences. There's nothing compelling for them to say, "I need to make this change NOW to make my business better." They're thinking, "Eh. It can wait. I have workarounds. Maybe some other information will pop up that will help me decide later."

The short term often wins. I was recently in a meeting with two key decision makers, a regional president and a chief sales officer. We were discussing various sales performance approaches and how they might match up to their needs. And here was the question they asked. "Amy, what's the typical ROI for these solutions? If my people will be out of the field and with you in training, how soon will we see results? Can we show something within 90 days?" I had to be ready to discuss their key success factors and confidently explain my recommendations on when they could see a return on their investment. I also had to be ready to help them articulate all of this to their executive leadership, so we could get a green light to move forward.

ROI expectations have become much more sophisticated, and our decision makers are having to deliver results almost immediately. Seeing tangible results within a quarter is becoming the norm. If your decision maker is considering a change and you can't demonstrate a meaningful return quickly, then they're likely to move on.

Commitments go beyond "doing the work." High-level decision makers are usually ambitious, with a lot on their plates. To grow their careers and influence today, it's so much more than simply "doing the work" of the organization. Your decision maker has likely invested extra personal time by serving on boards, or on high-profile internal committees. He or she may also take on other activities, like mentoring other employees, or volunteering for their kids or other causes they care about. And as if those aren't enough outside commitments, there's also contributing to thought leadership, creating their brands, and having visibility on social media. Today's commitments are much more demanding and go way beyond the day job.

KEY TAKEAWAYS

- In the new sales economy, decision makers are operating with lots of change and static; that means they have less time to think strategically about how to improve their business.
- Less time to think strategically about improving their business means they need fresh, outside perspective from thought leaders like you.
- The challenges our decision makers face aren't all bad for us. They're opportunities for us to find ways to add value, if we choose to see it that way.

WHAT CAN YOU DO NEXT?

- Ask your key customers and prospects to find out which of these challenges are at the top of their list. Commit to helping them solve that challenge—even if it has nothing to do with the product or service you sell, you'll immediately move up the value chain with them.
- Take time to understand your own mindset with these challenges, because you're dealing with them too in your life and profession as a seller! Do you see these as negative obstacles, or do you see them as opportunities?
- Grab a sheet of paper and list out the top three challenges from this list that you're personally facing. Draw a T-Chart for each challenge, and on the left side of the chart brainstorm all the ways this challenge is holding you back. Then for each item you've listed, try to reframe it in the positive, and then brainstorm a few ideas for new approaches. This will help you begin flipping that switch from obstacle to opportunity.

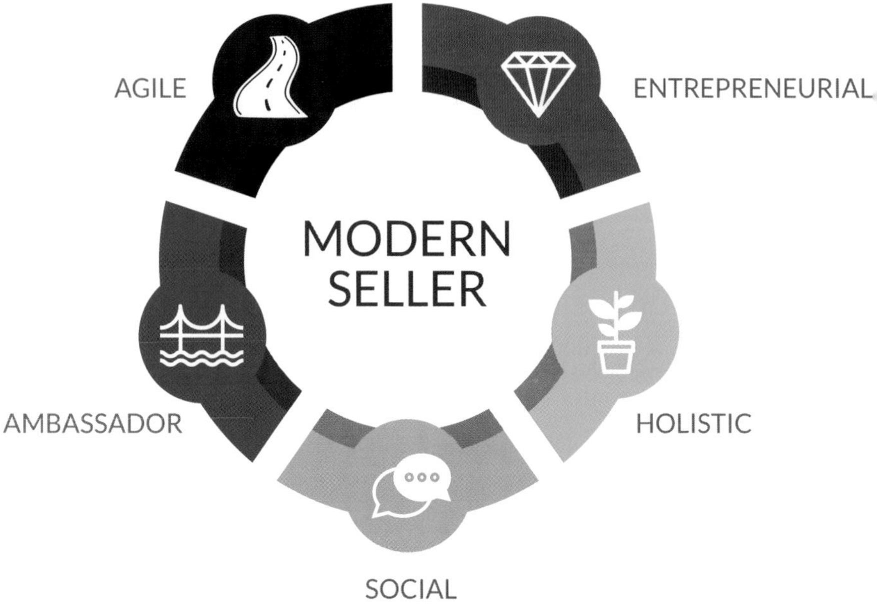
AGILE
ENTREPRENEURIAL
MODERN
SELLER
AMBASSADOR
HOLISTIC
SOCIAL

MAKE WAY FOR THE **MODERN SELLER**

CHAPTER 1

Because the new sales economy has radically changed buying habits, it's also requiring sellers to change their selling habits. In my sales career, I was fortunate enough to work for one of the most recognizable technology names in the world: IBM. Because of the logo on my business card, it was a little easier to get an appointment with a prospect or stay in front of current customers.

While I was trained to be a consultative seller, and I believed in the value of that, it was difficult for me to translate because I sold a commodity product line—PCs, laptops, and tablets. The reality was my comfort zone was features and benefits, product pitches, and conversations with mid-level folks. I was great at creating what I now consider to be basic conversations with my customers, and they liked working with me. But too often, low price, configuration choice, and speed of delivery won the day. I didn't work for a low-cost provider, which made it even tougher to compete.

The wake-up moment

Sometimes it's a single moment to spark change. My wake-up moment was around a multi-million-dollar opportunity in a large school district.

At the time, I was naïve enough to think I had it won—with the best configurations and the best features for students. I thought I had all the right relationships. My buyers were telling me that we were the front runner. I knew there was some competition, but I ignored it. I was forecasting this deal before it was won. So, it was a devastating moment when the district's board of directors went with my competitor, because they were 10 percent cheaper.

As it turned out, the board didn't care about product features or the logo on my product. They only cared about 10 percent cheaper. In this case, that 10 percent equated to half million dollars they would then use on consultants, books, or other things more important to them than computer hardware.

What I quickly learned was that selling this way wasn't fun or effective in the long term. At all. With that loss, I knew I had to change. Customers needed stronger reasons to buy my product, and I—as a seller—needed to give customers a better reason to do business with me.

This was also about the time where as sellers, we weren't only incented on revenue, but also on the profitability of our territories. In essence, my quota became my P&L, and I was the business owner of my territory. If I was going to be successful in this new game, I had to find a way to become that consultative seller I was trained to be. I had to become way more valuable to my customers than I had previously been.

What did I do?

This was completely new thinking for me. So, I decided to start with what I knew.

I looked at our product portfolio and pricing tools to identify our most profitable products. I looked at my business partners, and what the very best ones brought to the table beyond hardware. I looked at my peers, to see which ones did well year after year. I looked at my customer set in a new way. Rather than looking at just what I thought to be their *technology needs*, I looked at *their business and their goals*. I began to study my customers instead of my technology.

I learned my education customers needed to become more relevant and competitive on several fronts. They were facing stiff competition from alternative schools because parents had an increasing number of choices. Technology was advancing rapidly as students needed new ways to access their data, books, teachers, and even each other. To help students advance, learning was no longer contained to the classroom.

All of this combined into my a-ha moment: I had all the ingredients for mobile computing programs. Programs that combined the best hardware technology, educational software, integration, best practices, and support. If I could bring together those elements with my technology and the best business partners, I knew I had something none of my competitors could touch. This would be valuable to my customers because it would make a difference to their outcomes.

This was significantly different from how I operated in the past. I no longer just sold hardware. Now, I consulted with my customers on their mobile computing programs. My buyers were no longer only IT directors, but educational administrators, superintendents, and boards of directors. My goal was to become so ingrained in their success that my customers would want me and what I brought to the table. The technology would become more of an enabler.

My results changed dramatically too: Not only was I able to make my revenue number, I was also able to create a more profitable territory. My P&L was healthier because I wasn't selling strictly on price. I could target better opportunities, my close ratios were higher, and I went after fewer bad deals. I was getting referred to other schools. I created an entirely different brand for myself as an expert in mobile computing. My customers looked to me and my business partners for advice on best practices, and we had a seat at their table for strategic conversations. I had become consultative and high-value in the eyes of my customers.

In short, I made the transition to a modern seller.

I wish I could say this was an overnight transition; it was anything but. Change is hard. It took me a good year to fumble my way through the process. Lots of ups and downs, reverting back to old behaviors and making my way back. To this day, I'm still learning something new about modern selling. I'm still seeking out and creating resources to support the journey. It's why I wrote this book, so you could have these resources too. We know that today's decision makers face an uphill climb in affecting change within their organizations. Their world is so much more complex, their decisions interlinked to other parts of the organization. There's constant pressure to deliver on objectives, while keeping costs in check. Becoming a modern seller means the transition is always occurring, it's a continual process. The transition is well worth it though, because when you commit to it, you'll see yourself in a whole new light—and so will your customers. Your relevance will grow, as will your personal satisfaction and your results.

What can you take away from my story?

- If you're a seller, it means that to continue creating success, you likely need refreshed skillsets and mental models to help. These new skillsets and mental models touch everything from initial relationship building and prospecting, to how you grow your current customers, to how you handle the competition, and to how you position your value and brand.

- If you're a sales leader, it means that you also need to adapt. Take a closer look at the talent you hire. Identify new skills your team needs to be successful. Your skills as a coach will be more important than ever so your team can turn these new skills into results..

The Modern Seller defined

Because our customer's environments and their buying habits have become more complex, our skills not only have to keep up, they must stay ahead—especially in B2B sales. All this complexity and change means we need to make the transition to a modern seller.

What is a modern seller?

> ***A modern seller is recognized as a differentiator in their customer's business, and the value of their product or service isn't fully realized without them. A modern seller's customer sees the work they do together as strategic to their competitive advantage.***

Not every customer is ready for a modern seller, and that's why we should carefully select the prospects and customers who will realize the highest value in the work we do together. That's a tall order, and a very different set of outcomes than you may have worked toward in the past. Even in the most commoditized and transactional environments, there's room for the modern seller.

This isn't a book about sales tactics. While tactics like research, prospecting, presenting, and closing are all mission-critical to successful selling, there are lots of resources out there on those topics.

Instead, we're going to dig into the "skills behind the skills," the higher-order skills that will help us better execute on daily sales activities. My goal with this book is provide you with tools and resources to help you in your evolution to a modern seller.

Becoming a modern seller requires new thinking, and new ways of doing things to become that competitive advantage for our prospects and customers. There are five dimensions that every seller, leader, and sales organization need to cultivate.

1. A modern seller is agile.

Modern sellers are fluid thinkers who have developed a strong comfort level with ambiguity. Knowing things will always change, they can pivot quickly and confidently. They mentally sort and process lots of data, and then translate that into ideas that matter to their customers. They make strong decisions with the insights at hand, knowing they'll never have the complete picture and will course correct as they go. They create mental models to help them understand the current situation and anticipate new ones. They strike a balance between process and exploration, between structure and freedom.

2. A modern seller is entrepreneurial.

Modern sellers don't just have a territory or an attainment goal, they're leading a business. It's a whole new level of ownership. It's top line and bottom line, and the business becomes successful by helping customers reach their goals. Because modern sellers are leading a business, they're looking at both the current picture, and the future of where their business is headed. They're not just looking at the problems a customer recognizes they need to solve for, they're figuring out the potential problems a prospective or current customer doesn't recognize yet.

When I left a formal selling role to become an entrepreneur, there was a slew of new skills I had to learn, and all of them apply to modern selling. We'll uncover some of the key skills that will help you blend the best of entrepreneurship, leadership, and being the CEO of your territory. And, we'll delve into a what I call "stratactical thinking"—combination of strategic thinking and tactical action.

Being stratactical is being part thought leader, part strategic thinker, and part tactician.

3. A modern seller is holistic.

It's probably only in recent years that more emphasis has been put on the whole person, and it absolutely applies to modern selling. Modern sellers know their reserves of time, energy, motivation and discipline are finite—professionally and personally. Because of that, they focus on value over volume, and quality over quantity. They know which activities are strategic; they minimize low-value activities and other distractions. Modern sellers also balance performance with results because performance is the leading indicator that creates results. Performance is skillfully following through on the right activities that will create the results they're looking to accomplish.

Modern sellers also know that their own self-care is part of the success equation. They're better prepared to deal with the ups and downs that come with this profession. Self-care is a non-negotiable part of a modern seller's routine—a combination of physical, mental, and emotional aspects that makes them more successful.

4. A modern seller is social.

Social capital may never have a line item on a P&L, but modern sellers know their networks have tangible value. Social doesn't mean being the most outgoing person in the room or being glued to social networks. It doesn't mean relying only on social selling techniques either. Modern selling requires you to thoughtfully expand your networks, to cultivate and leverage them in ways that go beyond traditional selling.

These days, you're never more than a couple of degrees away from a decision maker or person of influence. You're never more than a couple of degrees away from being that person for someone else. Do you know how to find and make those connections, and turn kernels of a new relationship into a long-term loyal customer?

5. A modern seller is an ambassador.

Brand ambassador is probably one of those overused phrases, with a different definition depending on what's trending at the time. My goal is to give it a different twist because I see it as indispensable to the modern seller.

As I was in the early stages of this book, I was brainstorming with a mastermind friend of mine, Julie Holmes, CEO of Inline Strategy. She said something that has stuck with me: "It's not about getting the sale. It's about getting the right sale. Do you know your customer's aspirational goals, and are you sure they're going *with you* to get there?"

Julie is an example of an ambassador in modern selling. Ambassadors find the right customers, not just any customers. They know what their customers aspire to, and their customers are going with them on the journey long term. They innovate and grow along with their customers.

Think of being a modern ambassador as being a bridge that connects your customer's aspirations, your product or service, and you.

KEY TAKEAWAYS

- A modern seller is recognized as a differentiator, and as a competitive advantage in the eyes of their customer.
- Being a modern seller requires new ways of thinking and doing in today's environments. If this sounds overwhelming, fear not—think of it as additive! We're adding to your skillsets so you have more to choose from and implement depending on your situation.
- The most powerful part of being a modern seller is that it's about working on what you can control—your own mindsets and skillsets.
- Habits have compounding effects. Each habit we create spins other new and positive habits.
- This book digs into the higher order skills that will ultimately help you to better execute your daily sales activities.
- This book is modular, and it's designed so you can easily move around and revisit the sections that are most important to you. See a skill you'd like to work on now, one that will help you with a current situation? Jump there first and then come back to the others.

I.

THE MODERN SELLER IS **AGILE**

CHAPTER 2

From the Sports Field to the Sales Field

When I think of agility, these are a few of the words that come to mind: Speedy. Nimble. Fluid. Light. Focused. Confident. If you grew up playing sports like I did, agility is something you're probably familiar with. I remember hours of agility drills in the gym as part of practice. And just how much torture we'd have to endure depended upon whether we won or lost the previous weekend's game. As much as I dreaded these drills, they made me better during the game. It was as if my brain and body were better connected, I could more automatically respond to what was happening, and I could bounce back mentally and physically between each play.

What was once a topic only reserved for sports, agility is now part of almost every business conversation. Agile project management and agile software development are common methodologies. Change management is an entire discipline dedicated to building organizational agility. We're increasingly discussing agility on the interpersonal side when it comes to handling our emotions, navigating internal self-talk, and interacting with others.

A 2015 study by the Center for Creative Leadership discovered that one of the five most important competencies that modern organizations now require is *learning agility*. *Harvard Business Review* defines learning agility as the capacity for rapid, continuous learning from experience. Or, as *Forbes* author Kevin Cashman puts it, "knowing what to do when you don't know what to do."

Agility is something that wasn't even on the radar in the business sector as little as two decades ago. What this means for sales professionals and leaders is that learning agility isn't likely something we've been taught. But, it's something every modern seller needs to have.

Why it Matters

Why does agility matter for modern sellers and modern organizations?

Agility is an imperative for your customers because it breeds innovation and creates relevance. A lack of agility can take you down the path toward irrelevance, or even extinction. According to research conducted by the Association for Talent Development, the top indicator of organizational performance is learning culture. Ask anyone in brick-and-mortar retail about Amazon's impact, or someone in the transportation industry about Uber. Ask an aviation professional how Southwest Airlines has forever changed air travel. Chat with a film industry veteran how the digital era has virtually erased many "too big to fail" companies. Or sit down with a hospitality expert to understand how Airbnb and VRBO have changed the ways we travel. Each of these conversations will lead to the same conclusion: The new sales economy is an environment where innovative ideas can quickly take hold and upend the status quo. That need for innovation has also reached the sales profession.

Agility allows modern sellers to go deeper into business problems. One of the biggest differences between yesterday's world and the modern world is access to information. Our customers and prospects are getting baseline data on their own before they even talk to us. To earn a seat at the table we must go way beyond baseline data. Today's interactions require us to research deeper and know more—using that data to create original insights and ideas that will matter to our clients and prospects. Original insights and ideas prove our worth.

Unidentified problems matter more. Solving identified problems for customers, focusing on solution sets with specific features and benefits, or engaging just one single decision maker have given way to more complex solutions. Gallup's *Guide to Customer Centricity* refers to "buying centers" as the new normal. Multiple decision makers are spread across business segments, with various viewpoints and needs that increase deal complexity. Agility helps us to become explorers and change agents. We can better identify and connect the dots between players in the buying centers. It helps us uncover business problems our prospects and customers didn't know they had so we can better serve them and increase our chances of winning.

In a world of constant noise, agility helps us to filter and focus. For sales professionals and leaders, there's more on our plates than ever before. Those challenges facing our decision makers that I outlined earlier? We're not immune. We face them too. So how do we make more confident decisions about what customers and opportunities deserve our focus? How do we filter the noise so that we can make progress toward our goals? How can we maintain a sense of calm in the chaos? Everything comes back to agility.

Research conducted by Korn Ferry uncovered five key factors associated with agility:

A. **Self-awareness.** Knowing your strengths and weaknesses, values and goals, and how you operate in the world. It's an ability to honestly assess yourself in a way that's informational and not overly self-critical. I like to think of self-awareness as the ability to step outside of myself, my own thoughts, my mental "talk track," and try to see myself from another person's viewpoint.

B. **Mental agility.** The ability to look at problems and situations from several angles and figure out original ways to solve for them. This might include connecting data points in creative ways or looking for ideas entirely outside of your industry to tackle a big challenge. Or, it's a key piece of information that might seem to come out of left field, and applying it to a new situation.

C. **Change agility.** Having a high comfort level with knowing your surroundings and circumstances are in a continual state of flux. It's an openness to work with change, rather than against it. Change agile people recognize ruts, bust out of their routines, and don't get caught off guard when routines get upended.

D. **People agility.** An adeptness in working with and communicating with diverse sets of individuals or groups. Those with high levels of people agility typically have strong networks. They're able to move easily between conversations, and they find ways to build rapport and then more deeply connect. They can also quickly read and respond well to others' emotions.

E. **Results agility.** This describes those people who can take their collective and diverse experiences, apply them to situations where results are demanded, and deliver the goods. It might be a high-stakes turnaround or crisis situation, opening an emerging geography, or delivering a new product to market.

You've likely experienced the need for agility if you've ever had an experience that made you feel like you were thrown into the deep end of the pool. These are the often-formative experiences that we don't forget, because they're part exciting, part terrifying, and they push us past what's comfortable.

Maybe you moved around a lot as a kid, and had to adjust to new schools and new friends. Maybe it was your first professional job, or you moved from the comfort of one industry into an entirely new one. Maybe you spent time abroad and had to learn a new language and culture. Or, maybe you were newly promoted into a leadership role. Whether by choice or circumstance, each of those experiences requires learning new ways of thinking and doing things. It's our capacity for agility that determines if we thrive and succeed.

And, because these formative experiences are unique, you wouldn't have an *exact past experience* to rely on for guidance. What you do have however, are *previous and seemingly unrelated experiences* to help navigate these new waters. They won't be identical to what you're experiencing now, but your mind pieces together lessons from those past experiences and, combined with inputs from your current environment, help you forge the path ahead. You're agile when you're able to take in new experiences, pull out the key lessons, and then reapply those lessons for success in the next new situation.

What it Looks Like

An example from my own life on agility was my first professional job. It was an inside sales role working for a technology reseller that sold major OEM-branded hardware and software. I'd never been in technology. I'd never had a formal sales role. This was my first real adult job coming out of college. I had no exact experience to draw from in this new situation. So, what did I have to draw from?

For starters, I had an English and Communications degree. My classwork gave me experience in speaking, writing and successfully interacting with others. I wrote pieces for the campus newspaper. Several were long-form stories that required conducting in-depth interviews on meaty topics. Next, I was president of a major campus organization, and so I had developed leadership skills. Also, I had internship experience, having worked at a technology company over two previous summers and spent time in every department at that organization. I even experienced my first acquisition. The company where I interned was acquired by another larger company during the time I was there. Going back even further, a summer job I had in high school was cold calling and selling newspaper subscriptions.

Every one of these past experiences could translate into skills and behaviors I could use to be successful in this new sales environment.

For example, with my newspaper experience, I could ask better questions of my prospects and customers. I could also pick up on cues to help me dig deeper into understanding their challenges, so I could identify how I might help them. That cold-calling experience taught me how to pull myself back up when things didn't go well that day, or when I faced rejection. My leadership role, and the public speaking that went along with it, helped me participate more fully in customer meetings. I could work past the fears of being new and inexperienced. And watching the company I interned for go through an acquisition helped me better handle the changes that constantly happen in the technology industry.

Whenever you're faced with a new selling situation or experience, mining your past experiences and lessons will help you to also "know what to do when you don't know what to do."

I.

THE MODERN SELLER IS **AGILE**

CHAPTER 3

Strategies for Putting Agility into Practice

How do we become more agile? Here are some practical ways to build agility and apply it to your next sales opportunity or customer interaction.

1. Fill in blind spots.

Our brains are amazing interpreters and translators. According to a 2014 study by Radboud University Nijmegen and research done at the Center for Brain and Cognition at the University of California, San Diego, when our eyes take something in, there's ambiguity we aren't even aware of, some missing information. Our brains take over through a process called filling in, actively covering those blind spots and interpreting what we're seeing—in ways we can understand and do something with—all in an instant. Think about split-second decisions, like the swerve that narrowly avoids a bad car accident.

Or putting together a puzzle, where parts of the whole are missing and your brain is figuring out what it should look like when it's pieced together. That's your brain filling in the blind spots, making connections with pieces of ambiguous, gap-filled information.

Modern sellers deal daily with ambiguity. They know there will always be missing information. They'll never have all the details about a customer, an opportunity, internal politics, whatever the case may be—and they need to fill in the gaps to move things forward. They've developed a comfort level with their blind spots by making logical assumptions. They might fill in those assumptions in any number of ways: calling on similar experience, doing research, or having conversations with peers and leaders. The fill-in process isn't perfect; sometimes those assumptions will be right, and other times it will require a course correction.

Your customers and prospects are also dealing with lots of ambiguity. They're tasked with making decisions without all the information at hand. They're having to fill in their own gaps. So when they experience you as well-researched and confident in your ideas and recommendations despite missing information, they'll gravitate toward you as a differentiator. You're helping them to fill in their blind spots, and you'll become their trusted navigator on a path with lots of twists and turns.

How to Practice as a Modern Seller

Select a current customer or a target prospect you know is facing a big problem, whether it's an industry problem or an organizational one. It can be a problem your product or service helps to solve, but it doesn't have to be. Modern sellers think beyond their own products and services to help a customer or prospect solve a *business* problem. Your goal is to contribute strategies toward filling in their blind spots. This is especially helpful for working to get in front of tough prospects, or for getting yourself established as an authority in a new industry.

First, ask lots of questions.

- What information from my own experiences and background do I have that would be valuable in this situation?
- What additional outside research could help? (Think brainstorming sessions, conducting interviews, reading research from well-known thought leaders.)
- What are my known gaps? Where do I need to make some assumptions to fill them in?
- How can I fill in unknown gaps?
- Where can I go beyond what I know? (Completely different industries, disciplines, cultures, etc.)

Next, put yourself on a deadline.

Craft two to three strategies that will generate conversation with your customer or prospect. I've found it best to keep this exercise to about an hour, with simple strategies and some supporting information. Know that you won't be able to fill in every gap, or know if the strategies will work. The point is that you're crafting ideas with partial information and you'll ultimately test these out with your customer. Some questions to consider here include:

- What might hold me back from moving forward with sharing what I learn?
- Will holding back prevent me from differentiating myself with this customer or prospect?
- What's a logical next step after sharing these strategies? Will it lead to something that I can help solve in more depth?

Lastly, share them with your customer or prospect.

- Developing this skill means you need to present the ideas in either an in-person or virtual environment. Both are valuable skills to develop, for distinct reasons.
- In-person allows you to practice skills like eye contact, executive presence, and reading body language.
- Virtual allows you to practice skills like voice tone and pitch in a virtual environment, and deciphering how things are going, without the benefit of in-person cues.
- In either environment, you'll also learn where your confidence is strong, where it may need a boost and how you react to unforeseen circumstances.

Try this with three key prospects and customers. The knowledge you'll build will create insights that you can confidently adapt and "fill in" for each new situation.

How to Practice as a Modern Sales Leader

- Build a list of best practices from the results of this exercise. It can be shared across the organization, or it can be packaged into an industry whitepaper to use with customers and prospects.
- Leverage this as part of managing your pipeline. Ideally your team will uncover new opportunities as they do this exercise.
- Join a team member while they present, especially a new team member. You'll see where they're strong and where they have opportunities for skill building.

2. Develop strategic speed.

Research conducted by The Forum Corporation found that 90 percent of senior leaders considered strategic speed as critical to their organization's success. But less than half of those leaders considered their organizations to be operating with it.

The research concluded that an organization (or a seller) has strategic speed when they're moving toward their goals at a pace that creates value in both the short term and long term. It's the balance between the demand for immediate ROI and the patience to stay the course, allowing results to unfold in the bigger picture view.

In a *Harvard Business Review* article, "The Best Strategic Leaders Balance Agility and Consistency," author John Coleman argues for the importance of balanced agility and the need for self-awareness around our own tendencies. For example, if someone leans more toward an agility mindset, they're likely strong idea generators and have a high comfort level with change. But the possible risk is a lack of focus that can prevent achievement of longer term strategic goals. If someone leans more toward a consistency mindset, they likely have that calming, "stay the course" presence. The possible risk there is a tendency to become rigid or overly formulaic, which can prevent that person from seeing and acting upon important trends.

I shared that the short term often wins with our customers, because decision makers have constant pressure to show quick ROI on their investments.

In fact, several sales leaders I interviewed in the technology space shared that their customers have developed an "app-like" approach to decisions. Because of the need to continually innovate and low barriers to entry, they've grown more accustomed to experimenting with technology. Now, they're more willing to test technology from a bootstrapped entrepreneurial startup and not just blue-chip companies. This means there are more competitors in the space. They'll test the technology in their environment, and if meaningful progress isn't realized very quickly, they'll remove it and test something else—just like deleting an app from their phone.

Chances are, similar approaches are being adopted within your customer sets. What if you could be out front in these conversations from a business standpoint (versus simply a sales standpoint), guiding your customers? Helping them to know when to accelerate and when to slow down? Adopting strategic speed can make you that differentiator. It allows you to better assess where your customers and prospects may be, to know what's working for them, and to intentionally act upon what needs to be course-corrected.

Strategic speed doesn't mean anything if you're speeding off in the wrong direction. It's also knowing when it's appropriate to slow down, make sure the foundational pieces are in place, and then ultimately speed up.

An example of this was an inbound request that came to me from a global organization, interested in sales performance programs for several business units. The interest was driven by senior leadership, after the CEO presented to analysts that sales growth in higher-margin products was a strategic priority. How soon could I get to their headquarters and meet with their executives? How soon could we implement a program? Could we do it this quarter?

On the surface there was speed, especially since the request was coming from senior leadership and aligned with commitments to analysts. In reality though, this was one priority amongst many. And so, in short order it became crowded out by more urgent fires to put out.

Being a global organization, it was also likely that a solution and rollout of this magnitude would take time. It wasn't something that could be quickly implemented in a quarter. Plus, they were also going into their busiest selling season of the year. In this case, what may have looked like agility (supporting a quick pivot into higher-margin products) was a lack of focus (sales program being crowded out by other priorities). Consistency would be the better play. It made more sense to slow down, for me to offer other strategies besides training to help them drive higher-margin sales in their busy season. We could then use the time to strategically plan their sales performance goals and tailor programs to help them meet those goals.

This strategic speed approach is modern selling: I'm now a differentiator and I'm moving up the value chain, because I'm not trying to implement a solution before they're ready. Instead, I'm providing insights to help them succeed today. I'll help them pick up speed up later, when they're ready to implement strategic selling programs.

How to Practice as a Modern Seller

Think about a challenge you're having where things feel stuck, or a situation where you'd like to create momentum. Strategic speed can apply to virtually any situation: achieving a goal, tackling an internal challenge, moving a customer opportunity, building a target market, prospecting in white space, launching a new product or service, or building a new skill.

> **Brainstorm all the reasons why you may be stuck, being as specific as possible.** It could be fear of change, competing priorities, a process holding things up, or just not knowing what the next best step is. Spend time with this one to get as deep as you can on the why, to get beyond any surface reasons.

> **Think next about the bigger picture and the strategic relevance of what you're trying to accomplish.** What about it is strategically relevant in the long term? In the short term? Determining the relevance will help you decide on whether you

can create speed around it. It may be stuck because right now there's simply not enough strategic relevance.

Let's assume you have a situation that's of strategic relevance. Modern selling is about finding ways to be a differentiator, and being of strategic relevance will put you into that camp. Now it's time to generate some meaningful speed:

First, define the potential results and benefits—both short term and long term. It's important to articulate both. A focus on only the short term may result in speed but could have fallout because of a lack of long-term direction. A focus on only the long-term can create a situation where you're moving too slowly and not creating enough momentum to accomplish the goal.

Next, find alignment between the short-term and long-term list. Where can achieving a short-term result also contribute to long-term success? It's in those areas of alignment that you can then plot out your next steps.

From there, decide on what you're going to implement next and where you need additional resources to help you. If you're stuck on that next step, get some input from a trusted advisor or your leader.

This process can be especially powerful with large competitive opportunities and enterprise-level account management. It can also help with cultivating new markets where you need to make strategic inroads, plus work with and through others to accomplish results.

How to Practice as a Modern Sales Leader

Invest time in individual deal evaluations with your team members, with both a long-term and short-term lens. Take your team member through the above process to help him or her select an opportunity where there is long-term strategic relevance and a need to practice strategic speed. If you have a team of 10 sales reps, and each rep has one opportunity, track each of those to gauge momentum and close rates.

Get into the habit of coaching your team to think in both the long term and the short term by asking:

- What are the short-term and long-term business goals for this customer? If your team member can't articulate these goals, challenge them to uncover those first before trying to gain speed.
- What's the next step in this opportunity?
- Does the next step contribute to both short-term gain and long-term results for the customer? For us?
- Where are we stuck today or where might we get stuck? Do we need an agility mindset (pivot), or a consistency mindset (stay the course)?

3. Seek out continuous feedback and coaching.

I remember one of my early performance reviews, which as you can probably guess happened once a year. I was less than a year into my role, and had just won a very large account that had been with a competitor for years. It took a significant amount of time and energy to earn that business and I thought orders would be coming in right away.

Orders started arriving about six months after the initial contract award. And, while I had made strong progress in my role and even won a big contract, I didn't make my number that first year.

When it came time for performance reviews, I was rated toward the bottom of my team. As someone who is driven by high achievement and recognition, that stung. Not just the rating itself, but because I really didn't see it coming from my leader. I thought my hard work, my passion and my commitment would be a bigger part of the performance equation. It was a low point, and I learned some very valuable lessons that tie into what it means to be a modern seller.

First, performance ratings are an annual rearview look at results. They don't always take into consideration activities or intangibles. Modern sellers need to get beyond a simplistic numbers and ratings checkbox. Performance conversations should be regular, expected happenings between a seller and leader. Modern organizations have sales leaders who are coaches above all else. Their ability to coach individuals and the entire team, beyond the numbers, is what elevates performance.

Second, it was my responsibility to proactively seek out feedback and open myself up to receiving it and applying it. Modern sellers don't hide from feedback. They actively seek it out, not only from their direct leaders, but also from peers, other leaders in the organization, and from their customers.

I learned to get specific in what kind of feedback I was looking for, and who should be giving me that feedback. It meant I had to honestly evaluate my opportunities for growth. This kind of honest, transparent, and sometimes vulnerable self-reflection meant I had to separate my emotions and my reactions. This can be accomplished by creating what Harvard researcher and author of *Emotional Agility*, Dr. Susan David, calls a meta-view of the situation. In her research on emotional agility, David describes the meta-view as "creating space ... where you are able to helicopter above your thoughts and emotions, which is a critical human leadership and self-leadership skill." It's the space where we can take an emotional break, separating our self-worth from the feedback. We can then process the feedback for what it is: an opportunity to grow, to learn, to be better the next time.

How to Practice as a Modern Seller

Own your performance feedback cycles. Regardless of how often your formal performance reviews are, it's your role to seek out regular feedback. Set up twice monthly 30-minute reviews with your direct leader and make it a point to schedule them on his/her calendar. That early performance review I shared could've been make or break for me. I chose to turn it into a "make" and used it as an opportunity to excel. I chose to get beyond the numbers and into my performance.

Leverage your internal or external thought leaders. New to this role? Learning a new product set or customer set? Want to bust out of a rut? Schedule coaching time or shadow an internal thought leader to accelerate your learning process. You may want to get beyond your four walls, connecting with an industry thought leader who can provide you with a different point of view.

Win/loss reviews. Do you invest time debriefing your wins and losses to get to the key learnings? This means getting beyond the surface and into the deeper reasons. Many times, we're told that we lost due to price when in fact that's almost never the true reason why. Investing time to understand those deeper decision-making factors has so many valuable learning points—but only if we're willing to open ourselves to the feedback and use it to improve the next selling situation. You may want to leverage a third-party consultant to help your customers to share open and honest feedback, especially in a losing situation.

Consciously capture one new thing you've learned today. I keep a daily journal, and I write down each day one new thing I've learned. It may be a breakthrough with a new skill I'm working on, an insight into myself, or an observation about a conversation I had that day. This simple exercise has opened my eyes to the fact that I'm continually learning. Capturing those learning points elevates my awareness of them so I can apply them the next time.

How to Practice as a Modern Sales Leader

Yes, the numbers matter. But getting beyond the numbers creates a culture of agility. As the leader, you design an agile culture through the right feedback and guidance.

Challenge yourself to ask more detailed questions. Are your scheduled calls with your team members only for deal reviews, opportunity tracking, or issues? Instead, make your next conversation about that person, and learn what's important to him/her. Communicate that in advance, and the why behind your interest, so they can come prepared for the conversation. If you can understand what skills that person would like to build, or learn what they need to excel in their role, you're better equipped to help them as a modern seller.

Share with your team one new thing you're learning as a leader. Your team will respect your openness and vulnerability when you tell them one new thing you're learning or working on. For example, one leader I interviewed had to temporarily take over in a sales capacity for a team member who had left the organization. She was essentially filling in as a rep while she was hiring to backfill the role. While in the rep role, she missed a forecast because a client had pushed back an order by two weeks.

What she learned about herself was that in her leadership role she wasn't empathetic to that same situation with her team. Now that she experienced it as a rep, she had a different viewpoint. She realized she needs to handle those situations differently in the future. She could have swept that experience under the rug and no one would've known. But instead, she chose to shine a light on it by sharing the experience with her team, what she had learned and how she would change moving forward.

Make it a weekly practice to ask your team members one new thing they're learning. This one simple exercise will open exponential opportunities to infuse a culture of agility within your team. During your weekly team calls or at your next in-person meeting, ask one person to share something they're learning. It doesn't have to be work-related; it can be anything. Once they've shared what they're learning or working on, ask the following questions:

- What attracted you to what you're learning?
- What is most exciting about it?
- What do you hope to do with it?
- What connections can you make back to our work as a team?

You can take this a step further by documenting what the team is learning and share this across your business. This can be amplified if you're able to share on internal social networks or present these learnings to another business unit during their team calls.

4. Learn your patterns and know when to short circuit them.

Our behavior patterns, or our habits, are largely unconscious, and yet they're so powerful that they either make or break our success. Just as the brain has an amazing capacity to fill in details for us, it also stores all our patterns for instant recall.

The Power of Habit, by Charles Duhigg, describes that one-time conscious decisions ultimately become subconscious patterns. This is the brain's way of automating routine tasks so its energy can be used for higher-level tasks. The brain is wired such that we're usually unaware of our patterns until someone else points them out to us, we've hit a breaking point, or we wake up one day to realize the years' worth of results from them. It's these small, seemingly insignificant patterns that shape our lives and our success.

The question becomes then, do our patterns set us up for success as modern sellers?

The best way I found to understand patterns was what Duhigg called The Habit Loop. This loop consists of a cue, a routine, and a reward. The cue is the catalyst, whether internal or external, that kicks off the action of the routine, and the reward is what comes at the end of the routine. Do this exercise enough times and the loop becomes ingrained until it's entirely subconscious. Whether the habit is healthy and productive or unhealthy and counterproductive, it doesn't matter. They're all run in this same loop.

Duhigg also discovered from MIT researcher Ann Graybiel that these patterns, once formed, are never completely removed from our brain's wiring, but they can be replaced. The key to short circuiting patterns that don't serve us lies in consciously inserting new routines.

To insert new routines, we first must identify our patterns and our habit loops. Some of them we know right away, but many of them need a little more digging to bring them into our awareness. When we pinpoint them, we can then consciously decide which ones are serving us and which ones need a short circuit.

One example from my sales life is prospecting. I don't know many people who love to prospect (I think I envy the people that do a little bit), and I know I'm always happier when I've checked that off the list. Here's the pattern I've noticed: When it comes time to prospect, it's amazing just how many other things I can find to do instead, things that ultimately aren't high value. In this case, the cue is prospecting, the routine is doing some other activity, and the reward is a (false) sense of accomplishment from doing that other thing.

To short circuit the pattern, I decided to experiment with changing my environment.

When I changed my environment by getting out of my home office and into a different space, I found fewer distractions and became more focused. The cue is still prospecting and the reward is still the satisfaction of accomplishment, but the routine changed to help me get there. That change to my environment also had two other positive benefits: I dressed in business attire instead of casually, which increased my confidence. I also had to do better pre-planning so that I could knock out the task more quickly. Another benefit to short circuiting a pattern is that it often creates positive side effects on other patterns.

How to Practice as a Modern Seller

Get to know your sales patterns. Spend time analyzing your sales patterns with the help of your leader, a professional coach, or a trusted peer. The important element of this is the outside perspective, because we're often too close to our patterns to see them, or we find ways to justify patterns that really aren't working anymore. These patterns may include: how you start and end your day, how you're deciding on which prospects to engage, the way you prioritize your activities, your prospecting approaches, or your closing methods. You get the idea.

A place to start is dissecting how you start and end your day. Those patterns often dictate the success you'll have for the current day and how you set yourself up for the next day.

When you identify a pattern you'd like to short circuit, see if you can isolate the cue, the routine, and the reward. Once you've pinpointed them, experiment with ways that you can change up the routine. You may need to try a couple of different routines to land on the right one for you.

Create pivots. A sales professional I interviewed made a career pivot from technology sales into medical device sales, and she credits agility with helping her to successfully make that move. In her case, the cue was being immersed into an entirely unfamiliar environment, and the reward was gaining success in this new role as quickly as possible. Her routine became approaching each workday with the purpose of learning.

This included interviewing customers, shadowing subject matter experts, and investing in her own development. She reviewed her skills from her previous role, figured out the transferrable ones, and what gaps she needed to fill in the new role.

A pivot doesn't have to be a major career or industry change. Some other ways to create smaller pivots:

- Try switching up your physical environment to promote new thought patterns.
- Work onsite at a customer, or multiple customers, to get completely different perspectives. A sales professional I interviewed sells safety equipment to the construction industry. She makes it a point to regularly visit job sites, whether they are an existing customer or a prospect.
- Take a new route to the office or customer site.
- Talk with your leader about taking on a side assignment, one that's relevant to the team or the business and will stretch your skills.

Go broad. Going broad gets us out of the thought patterns we're accustomed to and encourages us to use different parts of our brain. This can be done several ways:

- Read books and other publications or listen to podcasts that are entirely different from what you would normally pick up.
- Take a class that indulges an interest outside of work. I've always wanted to learn another language. I'm fascinated by language and culture, so I took Spanish lessons and did a short study-abroad trip with my husband.
- Get out of the habit of always spending time with the same people and at the same events. Challenge yourself to expand your network by finding diverse and higher-level leaders to spend time with. Judy Robinett, author of *How to be a Power Connector*, calls this "getting into a new room." The broader our networks, the more connections we're able to make for ourselves and others. This expansion makes a difference

to growing our business and making more impactful contributions.

Get curious. In our eBook *6 Strategies to Maximize Sales Results*, my co-author Jen E. Miller cites intellectual curiosity as an "x-factor" for success in sales. She shares this statistic: "Research by Steve W. Martin, a business author and teacher of sales strategy at the University of Southern California Marshall School of Business, indicates that 82 percent of top salespeople are naturally more curious than their lesser performing counterparts." So, how can we foster intellectual curiosity?

- Carry a small notebook with you wherever you go (or use your phone), and capture thoughts, ideas, or that memorable point that someone shared with you. Also capture your unique observations about those ideas. This is especially powerful when you're at events. I'm always surprised at how few people take notes during keynotes or breakout sessions.
- Take notes at your meetings, every time. A study conducted by the 3M Post-It Brand team and Wakefield Research showed that "79 percent of executives think you aren't paying attention in meetings if you aren't taking notes." Once you've taken the notes, summarize the key learning points for yourself. Whenever I do this, I make connections and generate ideas I wouldn't otherwise.
- Focus on questions and not answers. Small children naturally operate with lots of wonder, asking questions about almost everything to learn about the world around them. Somewhere along the line we lose that natural curiosity. As adults, we tend to be more worried about having the right

answers. When we focus on questions we flex that curiosity muscle, learn more, and can identify new patterns or ways of doing things.

- Who do you know that's naturally curious? Jen E. Miller suggests reaching out to those people and asking to shadow them for a day of professional development.

How to Practice as a Modern Sales Leader

No Meeting Fridays. A client of mine has instituted a "No Meeting Friday" policy once a month, supported by the CEO. This creates space that would otherwise be overrun with meetings. Space is needed to uncover and process new patterns and ideas. That time is instead used for professional or personal development, or to dig into a new idea.

Work with your team to analyze their sales patterns. Help your team members to individually analyze their sales patterns, and see if you can help them to isolate the elements of Duhigg's habit loop. You'll likely uncover a wide range of patterns, skills, and learning moments that can also be shared with the larger team. Take this a step further by selecting a pattern that a team member wants to work on, continue to coach them and track how the change in the pattern is creating sales results.

Model creative questioning. Create a question bank for your sales team to reference as they're doing discovery with prospects, customers, or for use inside your organization. Even better, align the question bank to your sales process. Generate curiosity by getting beyond the surface-level questions that usually get asked, and go for the deeper, more thought-provoking questions. For example, a question like "What are the customer's business goals for the next 2 years?" can be tweaked to generate more curiosity: "What changes are driving the customer toward these goals over the next 2 years?" and "Why do these goals matter to the customer?"

KEY TAKEAWAYS

- Agility is rapidly and continuously learning from experience. It allows us to connect current knowledge to a new situation in front of us. It's a next-generation sales skill that every seller and sales leader needs to cultivate.
- Agility helps us to go deeper into business problems, be more innovative, and even uncover unidentified problems—all critical for relevance, both ours and our customers.
- Practicing balanced agility helps us to remain strategic and purposeful, because we can act upon necessary pivots while also maintaining a level of consistency.
- Filling in blind spots helps us to deal with ambiguity, to confidently and successfully move things forward. Our customers and prospects are looking to us to lead them through ambiguity as well.
- Working with strategic speed helps us to create value for customers in both the short term and the long term. It balances the need for short-term ROI and the bigger picture view.
- Specific and continuous feedback will hone your agility, and it's up to you to proactively seek it out.
- Uncover your patterns and pinpoint routines that no longer serve you; amplify the patterns that are creating your success.

II.

THE MODERN SELLER IS ENTREPRENEURIAL

CHAPTER 4

Employee or Entrepreneur?

Although it's been more than 10 years, I still remember it like it happened yesterday: The day I called my leader to quit my dream sales job—the one that I'd worked so hard for—to take the jump into entrepreneurship.

I remember feeling so nervous. My hands shook as I dialed his number. My heart was raced, and I could barely breathe. I even hung up a couple of times before letting the call go through.

When he answered, my mouth was so dry I wasn't sure I'd be able to get the words out. But somehow, I did. I managed to tell him I wanted to give entrepreneurship a try. I was going into the learning industry to become a consultant—to design and develop training.

I was pivoting into a very different industry (more on that lesson later). To his credit, he completely encouraged me. He made me feel valued at the same time, which is something I'll always remember him for.

"Amy, wow," he said. "From a personal standpoint, that's awesome and I'm really happy for you. From a professional standpoint as your manager, 'Crap!' I don't want to lose you."

And just like that, there I was, officially an entrepreneur.

It was 2007, and I was blissfully unaware of the impending recession. My emotions were a mix of total excitement and sheer terror. I couldn't wait to dive into this new venture, but I also wanted to go back to professional selling, which is what I knew. I really had no idea what I was doing, or what to do next.

I started out of the gate with one project, one client. What I did know was that I was going to do everything I could to wow that client while I figured out what to do next. One relationship, one sale, one client at a time created the building blocks of the business.

In looking back on the journey, people often ask what skill has helped me the most as an entrepreneur. That's an easy answer. There's one skill that has helped me more than anything else, and that's the ability to sell.

As I'd taken what I'd learned from professional selling to entrepreneurship, some themes emerged that I wasn't aware of before then. For example, many of my consultant friends had deep experience and expertise in their fields. But they didn't know how to sell themselves or their services. Worse, most didn't really want to sell. They wanted to do the work, but not develop the business.

On the flip side, some of my professional selling friends had different challenges. Some didn't take ownership over their territories, or want to develop higher levels of industry expertise. Some were stuck. Stuck in processes and infrastructures that hampered selling time. Stuck in their own approaches to growing their territory. Or some were stuck with bad leaders who couldn't—or wouldn't—support new ways of thinking and doing. And, while

I didn't know it at the time, this jump into entrepreneurship was a transition in my own selling mindset and approaches.

I've learned and experienced the differences between what I practiced as a professional seller and what's known as entrepreneurial selling. I first came across the concept of entrepreneurial selling in a whitepaper by Waverly Deutsch and Craig Wortmann of the Polsky Center for Entrepreneurship at the University of Chicago Booth School of Business.

In their model, Deutsch and Wortmann put the professional seller at the top of what they call a Resource Pyramid. They asserted that professional sellers tend to have a lot of structure and resources to support them—think defined territories and verticals, operations teams, product development teams, customer service, and enterprise administrative resources. They had case studies, existing customers, and references to help them sell.

Entrepreneurial sellers, by contrast, are at the bottom of that Resource Pyramid (and they're often holding it up!). Choices have much greater impact, and the sale rests on the entrepreneur's shoulders. Entrepreneurial sellers are selling themselves as much as they're selling their solution. Every day is a careful balancing act using tiny resource pools. Deutsch and Wortmann describe those pools as time, people, capital, and data. They use the word "scrappy," which has described me to a T since becoming an entrepreneurial seller: I've had to be scrappier, more driven, more resilient, and more resourceful than I ever had to be as a professional seller.

The bottom line is this: It doesn't matter if you're selling for a blue-chip Fortune 500 company (like I did) or a shiny new startup (I've now done that too), I'm convinced professional sellers and sales leaders need to incorporate entrepreneurial selling into their toolkit if they're going to succeed in today's business environment.

And if you're an entrepreneurial seller reading this, you would benefit from incorporating some of the process and structure of professional selling into your toolkit because profitable, high-value selling is what will make your startup venture go.

Why it Matters

So why does adopting an entrepreneurial approach matter to modern selling?

Your competitors aren't who you think they are. When I was a professional seller at IBM and Lenovo, I had a very defined set of competitors—other blue-chip PC hardware manufacturers. There were maybe five I kept on my radar.

I had lots of competitive data at my fingertips (compliments of a large marketing team), and it was relatively easy to keep these competitors in front of me. Apple was barely a blip in my universe. Google wasn't a verb yet. Amazon only sold books. Today, your competition is fuzzier and more loosely defined than ever.

For example, I interviewed a technology sales executive who routinely works with global Fortune 20 customers. Her customer set is dealing with an unlikely competitor, Uber. Not because they're in the transportation or logistics industries, but because Uber is successfully competing for and draining their access to talent. That talent drain affects projects and priorities at her client. That's left-field competition.

While I still believe inertia will always be your top competitor, your greatest competitor five years from now may currently be a tiny startup in an incubator somewhere, led by someone who is a passionate entrepreneurial seller.

Customers expect more creativity, better insights, and stronger business value than ever before—and that's just table stakes. The customer journey is a concept that has gained a lot of traction. I first became familiar with it while working with the retail industry. Research firm Forrester describes the customer journey as a "variety of touchpoints by which the customer moves from awareness to engagement and purchase."

I see the customer journey as the sum of my interactions (and my company's interactions) with potential and current customers, all helping them to decide if we should work together. It's a continuum that starts with a first impression, ultimately going beyond the initial purchase and into building a long-term relationship.

There's a growing body of research telling us that customers are a certain percentage of the way through their buying journey before they contact a service provider. Whether or not you buy into the data, the important message is this: Your customers are so much more researched than ever before.

This has come through loud and clear in my interviews. No matter where you find yourself in their journey, it's up to you to join as early as possible. If you're going to stay on their journey, you must bring more creativity, insights, and business value in early interactions. You can't come in with "canned" anything because it will give you away in a heartbeat.

The creativity becomes even more important as the relationship matures. It will keep you from falling victim to familiarity, where the customer sees diminishing value from your insights over time because they've come to expect it.

Commoditization and disruption require new markets and approaches to be developed. When I'm having conversations with customers on this topic, it usually doesn't matter what industry they're in. One common theme they're all talking about is that commoditization and disruption are affecting how their customers buy. This affects their go to market strategies and how they sell.

For example, the professional services firm that could predict revenue based on the billable hour for a specific service is disrupted by firms nimble enough to combine services and work on flat, fixed projects. The insurance carrier that could rely on annual premiums is now redesigning product offerings and seeing their revenue models change because of driverless vehicles. And the blue-chip software company used to selling shrink-wrapped products against defined competitors is now grappling with how to sell subscription-based software-as-a-service in a sea of like competition.

Staying successful in the face of commoditization and disruption reminds me of an approach attributed to retail giant Les Wexner. He may not be a household name, but you likely know a few of his global brands like Victoria's Secret, Bath and Body Works, and Abercrombie & Fitch. Wexner's approach is that the time to change things is when they aren't broken. The time to change is before commoditization sets in or disruption is so far along that you're finding yourself with a lot of catching up to do to stay relevant.

An ownership stance changes the game. Back to Deutsch and Wortmann for a moment. One of their contentions is when entrepreneurs hire professional sellers, especially in the early stages of their business, it's an often expensive and sometimes lethal mistake. I know this to be true because I've made that same mistake.

Why does this happen?

Usually because professional sellers don't take a true ownership stance. They aren't as passionate as an owner about finding a way to win in the face of objections and setbacks. Professional sellers who think like an owner of their territory take more accountability for their outcomes and success, no matter what's going on around them. They find a way, every time, to make their number. In doing so, they usually create higher value for their clients, higher margins for their organization, and maximize their commission checks.

If you're a sales leader, think about your team for a moment. What if your entire team ran their territories as owners? You'd likely have a team where every person is making or exceeding their quota.

What It Looks Like

Here are a few examples of what entrepreneurial approaches look like in daily sales life:

- An energy company that has been very successful in traditional products and distribution decides to add sustainable energy products to their portfolio. This is an entirely new and experimental market for them. Rather than build a full sales force out of the gate, they tap a small number of their top performers with entrepreneurial skillsets to create their go-to-market plan and begin prospecting for potential customers. Based on what they learn, they'll be able to determine how feasible their venture is and iterate more quickly.

- A technology sales professional selling into the public sector, where his known competitors are chasing the same large government agencies and educational institutions, identifies a niche market. He uncovers a niche market of technology centers that support smaller agencies and schools, and his competition is almost non-existent. He helps these technology centers become a strategic partner to their own clients, with offerings that combine technologies from his company plus those of his key collaborators. These same key collaborators now introduce this rep into their accounts. This new space is expanding his reach more quickly, along with his sales results.
- A key accounts executive is assigned to a single global customer, responsible for account management, plus identifying and growing new business. She currently sells into only two segments. Accomplishing future growth rests on her ability to create impact for her customer's business. As her quarterly business review with the customer approaches, she adds an agenda item to discuss several ideas she thinks will help them become more efficient in a key area of their business. These ideas address issues she has uncovered about their business and the industry, but don't seem to be on their radar. In this meeting, she seeks initial buy-in for these ideas to explore them further. If the customer moves forward, it will create more value for their business and more opportunities for her to reach her growth objectives.

II.

THE MODERN SELLER IS ENTREPRENEURIAL

CHAPTER 5

Strategies for Building Entrepreneurial Superstars

What makes an entrepreneur successful, and how do we harness it to grow our sales organizations?

There have been many studies on the traits and skillsets that make entrepreneurs successful. Entrepreneurial CEO Ryan Westwood documents several of those studies in his *Forbes* article, "The Traits Entrepreneurs Need to Succeed."

What became clear in Westwood's research was that every study turned up different combinations of traits and skills, with no one defined winner. In a quest for more clarity, he decided to conduct a study of his own in collaboration with *Forbes* and other academics. After scouring the existing research, they landed on 23 traits and skillsets to analyze, and then went directly to entrepreneurs themselves to weigh in. In total 2,631 entrepreneurs were surveyed, with each one reaching at least the $1 million mark in annual revenue.

Traits which made the cut as the top five were: vision, work ethic, resilience, positivity, and passion. Out of those five traits, it was vision that stood above the rest. Sixty-one percent of respondents cited it as the absolute top skill that determines success.

Entrepreneurs are lauded for their ability to see a need the rest of us didn't even know we had. When Steve Jobs stood on stage and introduced the Apple iPhone in 2007, few could have known how it would transform our lives. It has revolutionized the way we communicate with each other, how we document our lives, how we pay our bills, apply for jobs, travel the world and so many other functions. It all began with a man and an idea. He most certainly had a vision, and successfully enrolled others in that vision.

As sellers, that same entrepreneurial mindset to look beyond what's right in front of you and see the bigger picture will position you as more than just an individual selling a product or service. You're the founder, CEO, and chief bootstrapper of your sales territory. Your ability to create a vision for that territory will determine how quickly and profitably it grows, and your ultimate success.

As a sales leader, your ability to create a sales vision for your business segment, division, or the entire company has even greater impact.

How to Practice as a Modern Seller

Create your vision. It doesn't matter if you're brand new to your territory, it's been redefined, or you've had the same territory for years. Now is the time to create a vision for what you want it to be in the next year, three years, and five years. One technology seller I know covers a statewide territory that had no outside sales representation until he arrived. There were exactly two customers doing small levels of run-rate business. The rest—all several thousand accounts of the territory—were dominated by competitors. The company he represented was a virtual nobody.

His vision was simple: He wanted his company to become the most well-known and respected brand in the territory within three years—to be the clear choice for every customer and prospect. In short, he wanted to dominate the territory.

That vision translated into the strategies he needed to make it happen. This included strategies like go-to-market plans, key wins needed, and partner collaborations. But without first establishing his vision, he would likely end up wandering from one opportunity to the next without clarity. And when things get tough, those other four traits Westwood mentioned in his research—work ethic, resilience, positivity, and passion—become that much harder to harness without the vision in place.

Create your territory roadmaps. How well do you know your territory? The most successful entrepreneurs analyze their business from multiple angles. Your territory is a business in much the same way, and a territory roadmap can be your strategic guide. Successful entrepreneurs know and keep tabs on:

- Key wins and losses, and the why behind them
- The anchor clients they must win to elevate their brand
- Financial projections
- Customer churn rate, including which customers are of the highest value and which are time wasters
- Product mix and profitability
- The major trends, overall goals, strategies, and challenges facing their customer sets
- Who their best collaborators and business partners are, and they support those relationships accordingly

If your territory is fairly homogeneous, you can likely get by with one roadmap. If you have distinct industries within your territory, there will likely be enough differences where a separate territory roadmap will be the most helpful.

At the top of your roadmap goes your vision. This will steer your decision making as you grow the territory.

Look for the diamonds in the rough. Where are there pockets of opportunity that your competitors aren't pursuing? There are likely a lot of untouched segments that haven't been uncovered, or new ways of approaching existing segments that no one is thinking about. I mentioned earlier in the book about my experience in designing mobile computing programs. That strategy was my springboard to modern selling and to elevating my company's brand. It was something my competitors were doing in piecemeal, but not as a cohesive end-to-end program.

Analyzing other successful ventures might be the spark of an idea needed to uncover the diamonds in our own territory. What unaddressed need or market did the company uncover? How did they create demand once they uncovered it? What sales or go-to-market strategies did they put into place?

Circle the wagons. Is there an anchor account that would explode your territory's growth but is nearly impossible to crack? Maybe it's just mammoth with a lot of siloes to navigate. Or perhaps it's been an anchor for your competitor for a long time. If you've been in sales long enough, chances are good that you've come across at least one of these tough accounts. Circling the wagons is a long-term strategy you can employ. It involves analyzing that account to see what ancillary customers you might win first, and then building enough momentum that the anchor account needs to take notice.

In the real world, it might look like this:

- I interviewed a sales professional who calls on state and local governments. The state level is a labyrinth of agencies and departments with autonomous budgets and buyers. Many of them have been virtually locked up by his competitor for the past decade. Rather than use only a direct prospecting approach at the state level, he turned his focus to local county agencies. County agencies weren't getting anywhere near the attention from his competitors. This approach gave him several advantages. He was growing his territory through this local segment, and in the process, his happy customers were becoming champions for him at the state level. He then started getting the attention of decision makers at the state level, which wasn't happening before. He also has new leverage with case studies at the local level to advance his growth agenda at the state level.

Create your own feedback loops. Every smart startup works closely with their new customers in the early stages of their business. That customer feedback is vital to the success—and sometimes even the survival—of their venture. Feedback is usually direct between the customer and the business' C-suite. As organizations mature and management layers are added on, it's easy for those feedback loops to disappear, or at the least become less direct. Often, the result is customer frustration when things don't go right.

Even in organizations where there are formal feedback loops

and customer resolution processes, as a seller who owns his or her territory, you can become a direct connection between the customer and your organization. That direct connection can take a lot of forms. Here are a few:

- Quarterly feedback and best practice forums
- Providing access to product and subject matter experts
- Connecting your customers to one another—this is especially helpful when customers are solving for similar challenges
- Walking a customer through a formal resolution process and advocating for them along the way
- Scanning and replying within social media channels

How to Practice as a Modern Sales Leader

Adopt entrepreneurial thinking in yourself first. As a sales leader, everything begins with you. Your approach to your own territory will be mirrored back by your team members. Following entrepreneurial thought leaders in social media and other sources will get you into that mindset that you can then begin to cultivate in your team.

If you're already in an entrepreneurial or startup culture, spend time with your founder and senior leadership and learn what makes them tick. Then begin to analyze your own habits. Have you created your vision and roadmap for your territory and shared with your team? Have you shared your own successes and struggles? (You are after all growing the business along with your team.)

Work with your team members to create their territory vision plans. This can be a team or individual exercise through an offsite or kickoff event. Visioning and mapping can also become part of your onboarding process with a new team member. Especially in the onboarding process, new team members are in a state of overwhelm. A visioning and mapping process which combines some structure, along with their experience and creativity, will get them started on a solid foundation.

Create innovation and feedback loops within your team. In your one-on-one meetings, quarterly reviews, and team calls, ask your team to share one creative selling idea they've implemented with a prospect or customer. Or, have them share one tough problem a customer is working on or has successfully solved.

Setting aside specific time for idea generation and feedback loops will spark solutions within your team. You'll get valuable data on where your team needs your help to succeed and extend their ownership over their territory.

II.

THE MODERN SELLER IS ENTREPRENEURIAL

CHAPTER 6

Apply Supply Chain Thinking to Your Processes

The catalyst for this chapter comes from an unexpected place—an operations management piece on sustainable supply chain practices. What does this have to do with being entrepreneurial? The picture of entrepreneurship we usually envision is off-the cuff experimentation, maybe a little bit of chaos, mixed in with some Red Bull, and seeing what sticks over late-night games at the company ping pong table. It may not seem that entrepreneurship and structure go hand in hand, but they do.

Underlying any successful organization—startup or mature—are the systems to support it. Without systems, processes, and structure, everything's really built on a house of cards. Those elements need to be consistently monitored as a holistic ecosystem if we're going to create long-term sustainable success.

Stanford professor Hau L. Lee, in a *Harvard Business Review* article "Don't Tweak Your Supply Chain—Rethink It End to End," makes the case that if companies want to create long-term environmental and business sustainability, they need to evaluate their entire supply chain and apply holistic approaches to improve it.

Lee says it's not enough to just look at the end points of the supply chain, to make incremental changes, or make decisions in isolation. He drives home four key points in the article, all of which can be applied to sales organizations: the importance of connecting the dots between your own operations, reinventing your processes, working with your suppliers' suppliers, and linking up with competitors.

It's easy for sales organizations or business units to work in isolation or to make incremental changes. Examples of isolated changes might be tweaking pricing models, commission models, delivery methods, or product features. A tweak in one area can have unintended effects on other areas of the ecosystem and impact the experience we're wanting to create for our clients and customers.

Today's modern business environments and buyers require us to take a long view of whole ecosystem. Supply chain approaches can help us to do that.

How to Practice as a Modern Seller

Map your sales process end-to-end. It helps to take a current pursuit or very recent opportunity, and while it's fresh map out each step you've taken along the way thus far. This means looking at everything from prospecting touches and methods to how you qualified it, the buying roles involved, which internal teams and external partners are participating, and what demos or presentations you've done to date.

Don't leave anything out. This exercise will provide you with valuable data points and an honest picture of the efforts and their outcomes.

Once you have a full picture of your real-life sales process, now you can align it to your formal selling process, and more importantly, to how your customers buy. If you haven't mapped out your customer's buying process, do this first. Buyers have changed so much in the way they buy and in the way they want to engage with us, this process will show where you're strong and where there are opportunities to improve the chain.

When I moved from my technology product sales role (professional selling) to launching a training and consulting services firm (entrepreneurial selling), I had to relearn how my customers bought and how I chose to sell to them.

In my professional selling days, it was completely normal to participate in large RFPs that required many internal team members, with responses that were easily hundreds of pages long. In my entrepreneurial selling environment, I didn't have access to those types of resources, so I had to get much more intentional in how I chose to respond. If an RFP was part of a customer's buying process, I likely wouldn't respond unless I had a hand in advising on it and even writing it.

Map your internal operational processes end-to-end. Taking a page from Lee's playbook, map internal operational processes from end-to-end. He argues this helps organizations see the different connection points within their supply chain and find opportunities which can improve the entire ecosystem. I believe this same analysis can also uncover opportunities for modern sales organizations.

For example, when I sold a large order of personal computing equipment, getting the order wasn't the end game. Rather, it was the beginning of another process in the overall customer experience: getting thousands of pieces of equipment delivered to the right place, on time, built to the correct specifications, and in working order.

This was a complex international logistics process that involved lots of parts, sub-processes, and people. Any glitch in the chain meant we risked not delivering on commitments to the customer.

Once those deliveries were made, that wasn't the end game either. The right structure needed to be in place to extend the customer experience—onsite or virtual service and support, access to engineers, or my continued support. Again, any glitch in the chain risked our commitments to the customer.

This same mapping process applies not to just products, but to software or professional services as well. Modern selling requires us to look past the sales process and into what happens beyond it. How we navigate the post-sale process can mean the difference between a one-time sale and a long-term valuable client that sees us as critical to their success.

Creating a visual map of your various processes can help. Map out your logistics processes, delivery processes, and support processes in as much detail as you can. Include names of people in roles wherever possible because having strong relationships in those roles matters. For me, when something went off-track in a process, I knew who to call. I knew I would get accurate information because we were all in it together.

As an additional exercise in your mapping process, you might even elicit feedback from your best customers to help you with any blind spots.

Map your ecosystem partners and processes. With your sales process and internal operations in hand, now you can line up your ecosystem partners as part of your process.

This involves knowing your ecosystems: internal, external, and upstream (think the suppliers of your suppliers). These are the support systems that make things go, and free you up to sell.

In some cases, as Lee points out in his research, your ecosystem may involve your competitors. He describes a situation where like-minded technology manufacturing competitors had a similar challenge when it came to technology recycling and waste. Rather than create isolated and potentially inefficient business segments, they instead came together and created a singular company that focused on this effort. The result was an organization that served all these competitors and cut recycling and disposal costs across multiple countries.

Alliance firms are another example in professional services Alliance firm members are competitors in some cases and collaborators in others. They combine forces to serve a customer in a unique situation that neither firm may be able to take on individually. These creative partnerships extend the client experience and create opportunities which wouldn't otherwise exist.

These different ecosystem partners enter in at different points of the sales process, buying process, or internal operations. For each element in your processes, note the ecosystem partners you either have or might need to fill in any gaps in the customer experience.

As an extension of this exercise, you might work with a couple of customers representative of your territory and map *their* processes: buying processes prior to selecting you, and the operational processes once they've selected you. This will provide you with data points as to where you're providing value, and where there may be future opportunities to help them become even better.

How to Practice as a Modern Sales Leader

Roll your operations, sales process, and ecosystem maps into a common view, and incorporate into your overall territory planning. The average leader has a team of between eight and 12 people, and if your team members are creating individual process maps, it will quickly become challenging to manage.

To create more leverage, consider creating these as a team exercise during an offsite, or review individual process maps and roll them into a common, big picture view.

This does a few things for you: it helps you to better understand your team's customer sets (especially if you have diverse industry verticals), it helps you to find commonalities, and also to find weaknesses in the various processes.

Keep a pulse on changes to processes or ecosystems. For any tweak made to a process or ecosystem, there will be both intended and unintended outcomes. As you consider minor changes or even total reinvention, challenge yourself to think through the various outcomes. A team member, coach, or another leader can also give you different perspectives.

I mentioned earlier in the section that what seem like small, isolated tweaks to pricing models, incentive plans, and solution offerings can have bigger downhill consequences. In your sales leadership role, you might not have direct impact to change those things, but changes to them can have direct impact on you and your team.

Challenge yourself to change when things are going well. It's easy when things are on an upswing to let them ride. Or, when things are in a downswing, to try and recover through drastic changes. If there's one constant in modern selling environments, it's changing dynamics. Sales leaders who continually anticipate change and adapt will create sustainable success.

If you leverage the good times by trying fresh approaches, it takes some of the edge off the fear of change. When you do hit bumps in the road, experimenting with fresh approaches won't be foreign to your team. They'll be in a much better position to adapt, recover, and succeed.

II.

THE MODERN SELLER IS **ENTREPRENEURIAL**

CHAPTER 7

Strategic + Tactical = Today's Thought Leadership

Chocolate and peanut butter. Batman and Robin. Wonder Woman and Invisible Jet. All are things that just naturally go together.

Here's another combination to consider: Strategic thinking and tactical action.

Stratactical.

Two other things that are great on their own, but even better when combined in a modern selling toolkit.

Being stratactical is being part thought leader, part strategic thinker, and part tactician. This combination matters because to become that differentiator to your customer's business, that competitive advantage, it requires you to:

- Create fresh new ideas and insights that come with an outside perspective and deep knowledge of their industry.

- Draw connections from those new ideas to strategies that align with your customers' priorities.
- Turn those ideas and connections into specific actions that could create demand for your product or service, or help your customer create demand for their product or service.

Becoming the Expert

Thought leadership.

On one hand, it's a phrase that could be the center square in a round of Buzzword Bingo. On the other hand, when done well, thought leadership is meaningful for modern sellers. It creates trust, provides credibility, and even a little bit of fame in your industry. More importantly, it can help you to be of better service, and to make lasting change. It's a strategic path to building long-term relationships and closing more business with your highest-value clients.

Denise Brosseau is a thought leader for thought leaders. She's the author of *Ready to be a Thought Leader?* and founder of The Thought Leadership Lab. Her definition is aspirational and very applicable to sales organizations:

> *"Thought leaders are the informed opinion leaders and the go-to people in their field of expertise. They are trusted sources who move and inspire people with innovative ideas; turn ideas into reality, and know and show how to replicate their success.*
>
> *"They create a dedicated group of friends, fans and followers to help them replicate and scale those ideas into sustainable change not just in one company but in an industry, niche or across an entire ecosystem."*

I see thought leadership as the intersection of strategy, deep subject expertise, and selling skills. It's the courage to step onto a bigger stage, putting yourself out there to share your ideas and initiate change. And if you've done this over time with consistency and value, you have friends, fans, and followers (and likely a few dissenters too). It's also a drive to develop deeper expertise in your industry, and stand tall (but also humble) amongst peers, leaders, clients, and competitors.

For the modern seller or sales leader, the term "thought leader" isn't a surface descriptor or label. Thought leaders are leaders above everything else. Today's thought leadership needs both strategic and tactical approaches. Clients and prospects expect thought to be backed by action, by doing. It's strategic thinking and a point of view, combined with meaningful action. The ideas I'm sharing in this book are (hopefully) an example of thought leadership, designed to help you to succeed in your chosen profession—sales.

If today's thought leadership is the intersection of strategy, deep subject expertise, and selling skills, how do we combine these elements in modern selling?

How to Practice as a Modern Seller

Decide that you want to be a thought leader. It starts with the decision that you really want to rise above your peers and competitors to lead, and that you want to stand out to your prospects and clients (despite the discomfort). It means you're willing to put in the time, energy, and effort; you're committed to cultivating strategy, subject expertise, and your craft of selling in the process.

Develop your thought leadership strategy. I recommend Denise Brosseau's book *Ready to Be a Thought Leader?* to go deeper into the topic of thought leadership strategy and execution. She has created a framework for thought leadership which will help you think through its various aspects as you create your platform.

Specialize. Specializing is about very specific focus, and knowing which niche areas are ideal for developing your thought leadership and your sales efforts. Deutsch and Wortmann call this targeting, or finding "small and specific markets" that can serve as a launchpad.

You may be in a role where your specialization is pre-defined by product set or service, by territory, or type of customer. You might not have control over how specialized your territory can become. But you can find a thought leadership niche within that larger area.

To use myself as an example, while I had responsibility for a wide territory when I sold personal computing products (corporate and public sector), I found my greatest success in developing leadership on mobile computing in K-12 education. This helped me to be both strategic and tactical. I could share high-level ideas and I also developed the know-how of implementation. Those two things combined are what our prospects and clients need for their own business growth and competitive advantage.

If you're in an entrepreneurial selling environment or one without defined territories, you probably have more freedom when it comes to how you specialize. This means more choices, and the potential to become too broad. Targeting has always been one of my biggest challenges as an entrepreneur and I know it's caused me to take some winding turns. If that's your situation, I'd recommend Deutsch and Wortmann's work on entrepreneurial selling to help you through the targeting process.

Practice selling ideas to a defined audience. Like the idea of specializing, having a defined audience will help you hone your message and find that group which really connects with you. In the *Fast Company* article "The Golden Rules for Creating Thoughtful Thought Leadership," author Daniel Rasmus talks about how he advises clients to "go vertical or go home." Rasmus says people today (like our decision makers) "have limited bandwidth for new ideas unless those ideas improve their life or their work."

The best way to create and share the most useful ideas is to get as defined as you can. It will elevate you more quickly and help you provide greater impact. As you're looking at your markets, ask yourself:

- Which groups of people can I connect with—quickly and with impact?
- Knowing they have limited bandwidth, what ideas and insights can I provide that will help them improve their work or life?
- What's something useful I can share with the group in the near term, and how can I communicate it?
- How often will I commit to sharing useful and new perspectives to this group?

Commit to the craft of selling. While our thought leadership focus is related to the business we're in, we also need to remember what we're here to do: create new opportunities, develop new business, and grow existing business. That means we need to commit to our craft of selling, and it overlays our thought leadership.

In turn, thought leadership work becomes part of the selling and buying processes. This can be during early-stage discovery to create awareness and credibility. It can be leveraged later in the buying cycle to provide insights that set you apart from a competitor or get the prospective client thinking differently. As you're growing a current client, your thought leadership may open doors to other areas of the business or uncover a new problem you're able to solve for them.

How to Practice as a Modern Sales Leader

Champion company-level thought leadership. A big reason why your client does business with you should be because of your team, but there's also credibility that comes with company-level thought leadership. This might be whitepapers, webinars, conference speaking engagements, or subject matter experts available for deeper conversations beyond the expertise of an individual sales person.

One client of mine has created a formal thought leadership program. Individuals throughout the company contribute to it, and it's curated into educational pieces for both prospects and clients. Part of your leadership role can be to champion this broader level of thought leadership, and even encourage your team members to play a role in contributing to it.

Infuse thought leadership into your team touchpoints. Some of your team members may not see themselves as thought leaders. Some may be new to sales or their role within the organization, and view it as something for consideration in the future. During various team touch points and meetings, take the opportunity to talk about what thought leadership means and provide examples of it, both internal and external.

If you have team members who show the potential for thought leadership, they may become your team expert for certain topics or situations. This becomes a way to improve engagement and begin developing their leadership skills—today rather than tomorrow.

Coach to it in individual deals and your sales process. Because thought leadership is part of modern selling, it should play a role in deal coaching and your overall sales process. This becomes part of the daily conversations you have with your team members. This might also look like:

- Implementation of a sales enablement system that can route thought leadership pieces to prospects. The advanced data analytics available with many of these systems can show you exactly which pieces are opened and even which pages are viewed by a prospect or client.
- CRM-level checkpoints to note where thought leadership pieces have been shared in the sales process. This can help with deal qualification and identify business challenges at the client level.
- Opportunities of a certain size warranting time with deeper subject matter experts
- Invitation-only thought leadership forums for current clients
- Sharing how-to information with your team to help them develop their thought leadership skills

KEY TAKEAWAYS

- Entrepreneurial selling, combined with professional selling, is a must for modern sellers.
- Modern sellers are business owners. They run their territory or client base like a business. They own their outcomes and make it a priority to know every facet of their business.
- Modern sellers create a vision for business growth and success, both short-term and long-term.
- Think of your territory as a supply chain, and structure as your friend. Successful territories have the right underlying support processes.
- Each link in the supply chain affects your client, and any changes should be gauged for both intended and unintended effects. Never make changes to your supply chain in isolation.
- A visual map of your sales processes, your internal operations, your external ecosystems—and most importantly—your client's buying processes, will help you uncover strengths and opportunities for improvement.

KEY TAKEAWAYS

- Look for the hidden opportunities that your competitors aren't seeking out. They're "untapped markets" where you can create a name for yourself and own the niche.
- Modern sellers are thought leaders and their thought leadership is both strategic and tactical. They not only share big ideas and insights, they back them up with action and implementation.
- Today's thought leadership for modern sellers is the intersection of strategy, deep subject expertise, and the craft of selling.

III.

THE MODERN SELLER IS **HOLISTIC**

CHAPTER 8

The Non-Renewables

In my husband's family we have an annual tradition of baking Christmas cookies. For one weekend every December, we make dozens of different kinds of cookies. And because my husband is an engineer, he's always tweaking the recipes to see if he can make them just a bit better. (For the record, my talents are in the decorating and not the baking.)

Every recipe, whether it's from a mobile app or captured on an old note card in faded handwriting, has a specific set of ingredients and measurements. Each individual ingredient exists on its own but becomes something completely different when combined into a recipe and baked into cookie. Once baked in, the individual ingredients can't be separated back out.

This tradition got me thinking about what it means to operate holistically in a sales environment. Hopefully, our customers and prospects view us as a key ingredient to their success. That they couldn't imagine separating us, or our work together, from their outcomes. From a sales leadership perspective, when we're operating holistically the team works so well together, that the individual parts make up something much greater.

As I was conducting research on this modern selling dimension, I discovered that much of what has been written about holistic sales approaches relates to technology and digital integration, account-based selling, and combining various solutions or products that integrate into a customer's environment. These are all important examples of how sales organizations can combine separate concepts and solutions, forming them into a working whole.

It occurred to me that in all those examples, what was missing in the holistic sales equation is YOU. You are the key piece to the ecosystem. Without you, my definition of the modern seller doesn't work.

Living the definition of the modern seller means there has to be focus on you within the ecosystem, so you can bring your whole and best self to every customer and every situation. You the human being, not just you the sales professional or sales leader. Yes, your professional skills are part of your whole self. So are other elements—like mind, body and spirit—which when combined with your professional skills, contribute to your success and personal fulfillment.

It also occurred to me that when it comes to you, there are several non-renewables that need to be addressed for a holistic approach to sales: **time & motivation; discipline; and energy.** I call these non-renewables because in a given day we have finite amount of time, motivation, discipline, and energy. It's how we choose to use those resources in a given day that create our results.

Why It Matters

There's a real business case to be made for how the non-renewables can make a tangible difference on your sales results. The non-renewables help you to.

Create stronger relationships with your clients and prospects.

On any given day, you're faced with dozens of activities you could be doing. Prospecting, social media, CRM updates, meetings with clients, internal meetings, networking meetings, creating thought leadership, attending trade shows, following up on leads, writing proposals, working on your professional development. Then there's your volunteer work, your board service, personal projects, and your family needs.

The list goes on and on, and it's tough to integrate it all. These things usually swirl around in our head, vying for our focus. That focus can become so diffused that it takes away from doing something well in the present moment, including interactions with your customers.

When we decisively choose where to invest our time and stay focused in those moments, we're ultimately able to build better relationships with our customers. We're better listeners and we're more attuned to what a customer or prospect is sharing with us. We have more empathy for them. We're calmer and can think more clearly. We're more creative. These qualities help us to offer stronger ideas and more creative solutions. This breeds confidence and trust with customers and creates a relationship that's more resilient to competitors or internal inertia.

Elevate your executive presence.

Executive presence matters if you aspire to be top talent in your organization. It also matters greatly in selling situations—whether it's a high-stakes presentation, negotiating terms of a contract, or at a network gathering where you run into the CEO of your biggest client.

Executive presence is sometimes tough to define. Sylvia Ann Hewlett's book *Executive Presence* takes a research-based approach to defining it through surveys, focus groups and executive interviews. She defines executive presence as a "set of signals" that show you're ready to succeed at the next challenge. It's the "elegant packaging that attracts impressed attention, allowing your hardcore skills, accumulated knowledge, depth of experience and raw talent to stand out and draw others to you."

Her research uncovered three elements to executive presence: gravitas, communication and appearance. Gravitas encompasses your substantive knowledge and skills, plus other elements Hewlett describes: grace under fire, emotional intelligence, vision, reputation and decisiveness. Hewlett calls communication your "telegraph," and it includes your speaking skills, plus your ability to read and command a room. Appearance is your grooming and polish. But even more deeply, it's resilience and vigor—a vitality about you—that shows you take care of yourself, that you're capable on all levels.

It's that third element—appearance and vitality—which is supported the most by holistic approaches. It's tough to have executive presence when you're dragging yourself through each day, or you're suffering from burnout.

Maximize productivity as your most direct path to results.

Are you crazy busy, or are you strategically productive? We're conditioned to operate from the viewpoint that the person who is crazy busy gets the prize for sales success. Have you ever felt unproductive because you're not "busy enough?" If you have open space on your calendar, are you inclined to fill it? Has your drive persuaded you to pursue a new prospect or an RFP, even if they likely aren't the right fit?

Yes, me too.

These are all examples of busyness, disguised as productivity. Busyness is the long-winding path to burnout. Even if that busyness somehow helps us reach goals we've wanted to achieve, by the time we get there, we're so fried we can't enjoy it. More likely, it slows us down from achieving the *right goals*, the goals that will bring us the best success. The goals that will help us to hit our numbers, have the best mix of clients and be a differentiator for those clients.

Health insurer Aetna incorporated optional holistic practices like yoga, meditation and mindfulness into its culture with significant productivity results. *New York Times* reporter and author David Gelles details the journey in his book *Mindful Work*. Participants chose the practices they wanted to try in a three-month pilot, agreeing to self-report their results and participate in physical measurements. In both qualitative and quantitative measurements, Aetna determined that holistic practices reduced the effects of negative stress, lowered cortisol levels and improved sleep.

Not only did their health improve, so did their effectiveness. The program created productivity gains on an average of 62 minutes per participant. There were financial rewards too: additional productive time was worth $3,000 per person each year.

While holistic practices aren't a silver bullet, there's increasing evidence that they play a significant role in productivity and results. Imagine a sales organization getting back that amount of time per seller and refocusing that time on high-value sales activities. It will turn into new business.

Productivity is about decisions. Your decisions direct your present actions. Your actions today create future results. Productivity is also about experiments, uncovering what you'd like to accomplish and then finding what works for you to get you there.

What It Looks Like

These are a few examples of how the holistic dimension applies to daily sales life:

- The new business developer building a white-space territory with a new service offering—where right now there's a lot of rejection and more losses than wins. When he gets close to hitting that wall, he disconnects before the negative effects take hold. He goes on a run, reads a book, anything to take his mind off the stressors—that separation leads to new ideas and perspectives.
- The sales leader who coaches her team to prioritize their day according to their most valuable activities. She works with each of her team members individually to uncover their natural strengths and their priority activities, knowing that focusing on the right behaviors and activities will drive results.
- The account executive planning a complex briefing and presentation for a prospect, one that will make or break the deal. It's a high-profile logo, and a high-pressure situation. There's major focus from multiple sides—internal executives, third-party partners, executives at the customer. Her ability to determine her top priorities, stay focused on value, and exude executive presence will serve her well.
- The key accounts manager who is growing incremental new business within a specific account, because this account is part of his macro growth plan. Growing this account will create a domino effect into similar accounts. He's focusing his time and energy

here first, instead of diffusing too much of his focus elsewhere. He's getting beyond the single business unit he's been working in, conducting discovery sessions and building relationships across a broader ecosystem—within the account, within his organization, and within his business partners.

III.

THE MODERN SELLER IS **HOLISTIC**

CHAPTER 9

Strategies to Build Holistic Sellers and Sales Leaders

Time, motivation, discipline, and energy are the non-renewables, and with so many demands on our days, some specific approaches can help us to better decide where the resources get allocated.

Strategy No. 1: Time and Motivation—Invest time differently.
For all the things that we humans are capable of creating, the one thing we haven't been able to manufacture is more time. Time is the ultimate non-renewable resource.

In *15 Secrets Successful People Know About Time Management*, Kevin Kruse shares that the most successful business people, leaders, athletes and students all highly value time. Not only do they highly value time, it is typically their *top* value, even above health. I've done many exercises on values, and I have things on that list like freedom, health, relationships, making a contribution and meaningful work. But I discovered the one value that didn't make it on the list.

Time.

Hmm. That was eye opening. I didn't even really think of time as a value.

For everything we give our attention to, time almost never gets the value it should. It's usually something we think of spending, rather than investing. We can't see it, and it easily slips away. Kruse says, "We routinely let people steal our time, even though it's our most valuable possession. The magic number that can change your life is 1,440."

1,440. The number of minutes in a day. The same, equal amount that each of us is gifted with. What we value will get prioritized, whether or not we consciously choose those priorities. And, if we truly value time, then the value we place on time will drive the other choices we make in life.

Envision a typical week of your life. It may help to print off a blank calendar for that week so you have something tangible to look at. Look at your life holistically—your sales life, your personal life, everything integrated together. We all begin each week with 10,080 minutes, 1,440 minutes each day. It's up to us to decide how we fill that week. We get to decide how we invest in that week.

What are your choices? There are the big priorities that are almost never urgent—they're not screaming to get done; it's as if they whisper ever so quietly that they're meaningful, and they're waiting to see if you hear them. For me, this book is one of those big priorities. There's the mid-size stuff—big enough that you know they'll move the needle on something, but they often compete with your "big" priorities. The mid-size stuff often tricks us into thinking it's a big priority, because their voice is louder and more urgent.

In a typical week for me, the mid-size stuff may be knocking out some proposals or statements of work. It may also be something your sales leader or customer asks you to get done.

There are the nagging to do's that give you a quick hit of "satisfaction adrenaline" when you knock them off the list. Did you ever add something to your to-do list that you forgot—just so you can check it off? Yes, I've been there!

Lastly, there are the distractors, the stuff that keeps us from everything else. For me, it's endless email, all those articles I want to read, or surfing through social media.

How do you think most people choose to plan out their week? Well, for starters, they often don't choose at all. Their week plays out by reacting to what's happening around them. Their week becomes so filled by the distractors, the small stuff, and the mid-size stuff, that all available time is spent. There's very little or no time left for them to invest—in their priorities, themselves, or their team.

If we want different results or to amplify what's working well, our opportunity is in making different choices. What are some ways we can invest our sales time differently?

How to Practice as a Modern Seller

Lower your number of goals. That's not a typo, you're reading it right. I've lowered the number of goals I'm chasing, and I would encourage you to at least sit with this idea.

A year ago, I was completely overwhelmed with goals. It was to the point that I couldn't find my focus, my momentum, my voice or any results that I was satisfied with. It took a perceptive coach to point out to me that I was building four distinct business streams at one time: daily operations of my training and development business, writing this book, doing speaking engagements and building a sales consulting practice.

As a Type-A overachiever, it was painful to admit I had taken on too much, that I couldn't do it all at once, and that I couldn't do it all on my own. I learned it's darn near impossible to make meaningful, significant progress on so many areas at once.

As you're looking out over the next year, of course achieving or exceeding your numbers are the top-of-mind goal. But *how* you go about doing that as a modern seller may look different. What are the other goals you aspire to? Are they helping you to succeed as both a modern seller and a person?

My coach suggested that I create a list of everything on my professional plate and deconstruct my days. I was forced to make everything "audition" for a place back in my professional life. What I discovered was that there were many things I was taking on that weren't bringing value, joy or meaning to my life—nor were they helping me reach my goals. This included lots of activities I didn't even realize I was taking on—until I saw them on paper. I needed to first choose and then prioritize my goals, and this applies to sales goals as well.

This is an exercise you can do for yourself, by taking an inventory of the goals and activities in your sales life that are bringing the best results, and which ones are sucking up time and not contributing at all. Fewer goals can actually help you accelerate your results.

Look at your time from both macro and micro levels. Along with a laser focus on your goals, looking at your time from the macro level is a life-changing way to approach your relationship with time. Most of us get caught up in the micro, what's right in front of us, at the expense of envisioning the bigger picture. But the micro still matters, because it's in our daily activities that we eventually achieve that big picture.

The macro level includes analyzing your territory and creating that vision of what you want it to look like in three-to-five years. One sales professional I interviewed onboarded into a new role for a technology company. His territory had just a couple of big customers (that everyone was trying to do business with) and lots and lots of white space. The territory was underperforming but had huge potential. He knew that with two big customers, all it took was one not producing to completely derail it. He had a choice to make on where to invest his time.

A micro-level approach might say to exclusively invest time with those two large customers and try to keep the competition out. A macro-level view would show a broader perspective. For example, investing time in finding the gems in that white space that competitors aren't investing in—a longer-term strategy for sure, but ultimately one that turned the territory around. In three years, it went from only those two large customers to a portfolio of over 100 customers. These customers also refresh their technology every three-to-five years, so it creates an annuity stream for the client base.

Macro time planning could also include planning for your half or quarter, based on your annual quota or other big picture goals. This could mean conversations around account planning, white-space growth, key wins, collaboration, and skills you need to get to your goals. That macro level is necessary so when we get into the daily grind of sales activities, we still have that strategic picture to visualize.

Looking at time from the micro level could include your daily activities. Determine the most high-value activities that when done each day, add up over time. As you're planning at the micro-level, align each activity to a macro-level goal so you can visualize the direct tie between this activity and the bigger picture.

Work with your personal style and the tools that will improve your odds of it becoming habit. I personally like a low-tech visual that I color code. It helps me to better process how I'm investing my time, and I can quickly see if I'm dedicating time to what I'm saying are my priorities.

Remove one thing from your calendar today or this week. Each of us has something on the calendar that we just don't need to be doing—whether it's because we lack the skill or ambition to complete it, or it's out of alignment with our goals. If you can find one thing on your calendar today that you're able to delegate or delete, you can free up that time to invest differently. I use the words "today" and "this week" to intentionally keep this activity in the present; not something to do next week, or next month. It's so easy for unintentional meetings and activities to land on my calendar that I've found I need to keep this activity front and center.

Get to know your most productive times of the day, and then commit to getting your most relevant task done in that time. Maybe it's prospecting, or preparing for a customer presentation, or writing a thought leadership piece. Setting a timer does wonders for my focus, because I know that time is dedicated to making forward progress on that one thing and nothing else. It usually keeps me from distractions, because I know after that set time, I'm going to get a break. In fact, I have a timer going right now.

Batch your tasks wherever you can, whether personal or professional. Something magical happens when we batch our tasks. Our brain gets into a rhythm with those tasks, we become more productive, and we get better at the task. Because batching helps me to stay focused, it's also a huge time saver. I'm not moving from one thing to the next and disrupting my workflow.

Create unscheduled time, even if it's 30 minutes a day, just to think. We live with constant streams of data and information, which instead of helping us, can send us into an overloaded state and reduce our ability to make decisions. In *Smarter Faster Better, The Secrets of Being Productive in Life and Business*, author Charles Duhigg explains this as a concept called information blindness. There's a tipping point to how much information is valuable, before it becomes a detractor and our decisional compass starts going haywire.

The antidote to that is creating space and silence to hear our own voices and process our thoughts. This means turning off devices, getting out of the office and getting into a place where your mind can wander and free associate. *(If you've read the section on learning agility, this unscheduled time is also crucial to that skillset.)*

Shorten every meeting you control by 25 percent. This is a practical way to add hours to your time investment bank. Who invented the hour increment for meetings anyway? Does that meeting really need a full hour? See if you can get it done in a meaningful way in 45 minutes. I recently had a 30-minute scheduled Skype conversation that lasted just 22 minutes. When you're a master of your time, a side benefit is that it also creates credibility. When you need more time with internal teams or with customers, they know that you're requesting that time because it's needed and not because it was an increment in your calendar.

How to Practice as a Modern Sales Leader

Approach your team goal setting differently. I'm on the board of directors for an organization with 22 board members. When it came to goal setting for board members, our initial approach was centered around individual goals, with each of us independently setting two goals. I led the committee in charge of tracking our progress. Doing some quick math, that spiraled to 44 goals that became diluted and untrackable. I'd say we achieved less than five percent of those goals, and the ones that were achieved, if we're being honest, didn't create any big impact. As the leader, I was accountable to those results.

That lesson helped us to take a different approach. We're now focused on one larger, more courageous goal that also leverages our individual time and talents. We can now rally around the goal, track progress more easily and envision the impact we'll have when we reach that goal—together.

Similarly, sales is often viewed as a set of individual contributions that make up a larger goal. But what would your team look like if there was one big goal you were committed to achieving together, in addition to individual quotas? The key is something meaningful. When time is invested, it matters to everyone and there is an impactful payoff.

Rethink individual development plans. At the individual level, consider lowering the number of goals your team members are putting into their development plans. Most of us can tackle one or two big goals each year, broken down into smaller tasks. This may not sound like a lot. But, when they're meaningful, they create much more momentum than lots of smaller goals.

Let's say you're leading a team of 10 people (the average team is between eight and 12 people). Imagine the power of time invested into 10 meaningful goals to the business. And the time saved in not chasing three times as many little goals, just to fill up a development plan.

Leverage macro planning and micro planning in each team member's territory. Ask each team member to develop a macro plan for their territory, and then micro plan activities. This is an opportunity to brainstorm and be creative. How can we take different approaches from the past? Different approaches from our competitors? What's untapped? What's working well that we can amplify in other territories? How can we better leverage our ecosystem of resources?

This exercise considers your long-term growth goals, and not just the quarter-by-quarter snapshot we're so used to tracking for shareholders. Envision sharing with senior leadership the macro plans for your geography, in which each of your team members has an ownership stake. While each macro plan may have some "blue sky" elements to it, it will also be grounded in micro planning, because you took the time to lay out the high-value activities that will pave the path.

Strategy No. 2: Discipline—Live from a different set of lists.

I'm looking around at my desk right now and I can see at least three different lists I'm keeping. I'm sure some of them have overlap, because I'm always starting new lists. On paper. On my phone. In my head.

There's a saying that you teach what you most need to learn. So, as you can tell, I have some work to do on the lists I keep.

I wish I could say by reading this section that the usual to-do list would completely go away. But I'd like to get us thinking differently about how we prioritize our activities and suggest other lists we may want to keep as modern sellers and leaders.

I've compiled a pretty long list for you (pun intended). To keep it easy, I recommend picking the one or two that speak to you the most right now and experiment with them. See what works for you and integrates well into your daily life.

Modern Leadership Lists

These are modern lists that I keep "old style" on 3x5 notecards. They have a specific place in my office; I look at them a few times a year, or when I'm doing strategic visioning and planning. They change and evolve as I change and evolve. I like to think of them as my true north, helping me stay oriented to what I most value.

Be. I first heard of the "To Be" list while I was at a leadership event several years ago. As someone who is a natural "doer" and is energized by activity, this list always stuck with me. Most modern sellers have high ambition, and what comes along with that are usually long lists of things to do. Angel investor John Huston introduced me to the concept of being versus doing, and shared that this is usually a much shorter and more thoughtful list to create. What kind of person do I want to be? What kind of leader do I want to be? Who do I want to be as a modern seller? What attributes do I value the most and want to develop in myself? These are the bigger questions to answer that can ultimately drive what we do daily.

Have. Not necessarily in the material sense, but instead: What kind of experiences do I want to have? What kind of relationships? What do I want to create with my talents and skills? What do I want others, including my customers, to have because of their relationship with me?

For example, in your modern selling career you want may want to experience international sales, or experience another aspect of your organization, or new customer verticals. You may want to experience sales leadership or create mentoring relationships.

Achieve. Modern sellers and leaders are no doubt an achievement-oriented bunch, and I'm in that same camp. With that said, your quota may take the first spot on this list. After that, give some thought to strategic achievements that are important to your individual growth and, in a bigger sense, your legacy.

In what ways can you channel that ambition, that speaks to your basic human need to contribute? This book has been on my Achieve list for a while. I see it as an achievement on many fronts. First, it's a professional achievement. It will help to grow my business and platform. More importantly, I hope it contributes to my legacy of wanting to inspire others to grow, to push past what's comfortable, and to step into being their best leader.

Serve. What gives you the most charge when you think about serving beyond yourself? What people, groups or organizations do you gravitate toward? What service can you step into that pushes you out of your comfort zone? These may be both personal and professional experiences, and I often like to combine the two where I can.

When I started my company, I quickly realized that I needed to find an outlet that spoke to my need to connect and serve, but also build skills and grow my business in my chosen field. I chose an organization that focused on talent development and leadership, and then I found the most impactful committee I could, the programming committee. I raised my hand to lead that committee, which involved interacting with local corporate leaders, as well as other experts and practitioners in the industry.

That opportunity to serve helped me develop new skills in training program development, marketing, and public speaking. It allowed me to make connections I still have today and ultimately led to growing my business.

What are one or two organizations that can help you accomplish those same things? When we narrow our focus, we can create more exponential results. When you find these opportunities, don't just join—dive in and volunteer.

Stretch. Your stretch list has those things on it that scare you just a bit (in a good way) when you read through them. They're uncomfortable, they challenge you. One of my stretch goals is to become fluent in Spanish. My husband and I took Spanish lessons and then spent time in immersion, traveling to Mexico to live with a local family and continue our studies.

What I learned from that experience still helps me today in the sales profession. Getting uncomfortable in those moments made me a stronger person, I'm more resilient. I can build relationships in other cultures. I can imperfectly stumble through something that is difficult and learn from it. And getting out of what's comfortable can be fun and enjoyable. As humans, we have a need to progress and move forward, and a stretch list can help you do that.

Not do. This is a list that we've probably seen in other places and from well-known gurus. But it's worth repeating, because how many times are we doing things that we just shouldn't or don't want to be doing? How many times do we do things, almost subconsciously, and then realize we've lost an entire productive day? Because this book is a top priority for me right now, I want to dedicate my most energetic time to it. Which for me, is usually in the morning. So that means I've had to shift a few things around. On my current not do list:

- Don't take morning meetings on specific days of the week
- Don't spend more than 30 minutes in the morning on email
- Don't accept meetings where I'm not absolutely needed (I instead work to delegate)
- Don't work past 6 p.m.
- Don't bid on or say yes to projects that don't meet certain criteria.

If this is something new for you, I encourage you to try this one on. See how it can help you to stay focused on your most important selling priorities or defined goals.

Modern Selling Lists

These are the lists that can help you focus on your most important activities and elevate your productivity. Several of these can be used in collaboration with your CRM, and can give you that extra boost of focus.

Daily Priority. *The One Thing* authors Gary Keller and Jay Papasan share the strategy of investing the first part of your day working on your top priority, the one that will move you forward in a significant way. Can you look at your day, and know the one or two priority activities that are "must accomplish" for your sales day? The days when I do this, I'm measurably more productive because I've chosen to focus my energies and make meaningful progress on a smaller number of items.

Top 25 Prospects. This is a list of company-level prospects that are considered your top tier. While your CRM might maintain all your prospects, this view helps keep your priority prospects top of mind. Within each of those company-level prospects, list out the key buying roles and individuals that you need to reach. Consider categorizing further by the strength of the relationship and other centers of influence. This will give you a visual into the progress you need to make within each prospect.

Daily Prospecting. As a companion to your Top 25 Prospects, this is a list of your daily prospects you need to reach. This list should be created the evening before, so it's ready to go for your prospecting block. It also helps to segment the list in ways that will help you create momentum. For example, you may segment by industry, at company-level or by prospecting method. I gain the most momentum by sticking to a single prospecting method in a block — for example, one block of time is dedicated only to phone calls.

Centers of Influence. This is a list of the well-connected individuals and leaders in your network that you need to establish relationships with to collaborate, idea share, conduct research or learn from. They're the people you're introduced to through others. This list is critical to extending your reach and your opportunities. For example, my board service peers and my university alumni are Centers of Influence.

Follow up. Very few sales professionals have systemized follow-up, even with their CRMs tracking it for them. It takes commitment to follow up, and follow up and follow up. I'm guilty of it too, which is why this topic made the list. I typically segment this from my prospect list to keep it cleaner and shorter. This list includes follow-up after things like initial meetings, keynote engagements, presentations, networking events, coffees and board meetings.

Learning. Your own development time will elevate you from the rest of your peers and competitors. What's on your learning list? It can be sales-related, or if you've already read the section on agility, your list may now be broader. I'm a bit of a learning junkie, so it helps me to keep this list cleaned up and organized into one or two key themes.

Ideas. Those flashes of brilliance that come to you in random places? They need to get written down somewhere, as soon as they pop into your head. I keep a notebook in my bag, on my nightstand and on my desk. I write down any idea that comes to me, no matter how silly or insignificant it may seem. The simple act of getting it out of your brain and onto paper allows it to unfold and gives you a chance to validate it before it's forgotten. I clean out this list periodically so old ideas don't crowd out the new ones. If you prefer high-tech, there are a lot of apps out there that can help you keep and track your ideas.

Trigger events. Trigger events are those point-in-time events happening in the industry or at your customers that can provide just the opening you need to get in the door. I highly recommend *Selling to Big Companies* by Jill Konrath for more on this topic. Like ideas, trigger events can be easily lost and forgotten. But they can be a top source of urgent needs happening at a current client or prospect. When you see a trigger event, capture it, and then determine if it's worth following up on. If it is, it can make its way to your prospecting or follow-up lists.

Win/Loss List. How many times do we either win or lose a deal, and then really take the time to understand why? We're so busy, it's easy to brush right past a win or loss and take only the surface-level learning points. But we never dig deeper into it. It's where the best information is to help us understand what's working or not working—with sales processes, business processes, talent and skills. To make the most of this list, take your most recent win and your most recent loss, and dissect them around the end-to-end experience from both your perspective and your customer's perspective.

Failure list. The failure list is the brainchild of Dr. Tina Seelig, professor at Stanford University, who was interviewed by author Dan Pink on his PinkCast. She encourages her students to keep a daily failure list, writing down at least one thing that they messed up, whether tiny or epic. Along with that one thing they messed up, they need to write down what they learned from the experience. This accomplishes two key things. First, it uses failure as a data point to learn from, and it takes the stigma out of making mistakes. If we aren't making mistakes, then we aren't putting ourselves out there, we aren't progressing. Second, when we write down the mistake, along with what we've learned from it, we're less likely to repeat it. Try keeping a failure list of your mistakes made in selling. Use them as data points for improvement, and see what you can learn for the next opportunity.

How to Practice as a Modern Seller

Select one leadership list and one modern selling list to incorporate into your life. Let your sales leader know which ones you've selected. I've found the best way to make these lists "stick" is to tie them to something important. Decide on the lists that will help you close more business, reach that stretch goal, get the promotion—whatever inspires you to step into your next level of modern-selling success.

Work the lists consistently for 90 days. How long does it take to create a habit? There's varying information on the exact number. My completely unscientific theory is that a good three months can usually form the basis of a habit, and it will depend on how much change the new habit is creating. Give yourself some time and space to get consistent with the lists you've chosen, and depending on the lists, decide what consistent looks like for you. From there, you can decide to keep those lists, tweak them or select new lists.

How to Practice as a Modern Sales Leader

As a modern sales leader, I encourage you to do the same thing as what I've suggested for the modern seller. You're likely just as crazy busy as they are, but multiplied by the performance requirements and results of an entire team. You're also responsible for modeling by example. If you're doing this work also and talking about it, you're more likely to get your team focused on the right lists. Some other ideas for how to use these lists with your team:

- Incorporate conversations about these lists during your cadence calls.
- Tie these lists to performance conversations to help your team see the correlation of this work to their results.

- Select a "list of the quarter." Pick one of these lists that would most benefit the team in their sales goals, implement it, and coach to it for a quarter.

Strategy No. 3: Energy—Cultivate resilience.

In early 2015, I was in full-on growth mode in my business, driving toward the "next level" of success. All the outside signs of success were there: We were adding new team members, winning bigger client engagements, getting more visibility and recognition for our work. But there was something underneath that outside success that wasn't quite right.

I was working like crazy. There was no getting away from work. Even when I wasn't working, my mind was still working—thinking about the business 24/7. I couldn't turn it off. That eventually created a complete lack of excitement over client projects. I lost the mojo and the discipline to prospect. I had that feeling of dread on Sunday evenings before heading into another crazy work week. Selling stopped being fun and I was running on empty. It was affecting my ability to close new business, take care of current clients, and to lead. It's tough enough when you're an employee, but even more so when you're the CEO and the owner. I didn't realize it at the time, but those were all signs of impending burnout.

Executive coach Monique Valcour describes three components to watch for in her *Harvard Business Review* article "Beating Burnout."

The first component is exhaustion. Think of how you feel dragging yourself out of bed in the morning after only a few hours of sleep. Even after just a day or two of this, you feel the effects. A sign of exhaustion is that "tired in your bones" feeling that won't go away, even with good sleep.

The second component is cynicism. Cynicism goes deeper than negativity—it's a sense of disconnection, isolation, or apathy about your work or your environment.

The third component is inefficacy, a feeling that no matter how productive or skilled you are, it's not enough anymore. It's a loss of confidence in our skills or abilities to perform, even if there isn't tangible evidence of that happening.

Burnout is getting more attention as something very real, beyond what we typically think of as everyday stressors. Sales is a pressure cooker of performance, expectations and results. It's the only profession I know of where your results are right in front of you every day. Knowing if you're headed toward burnout means figuring out if the symptoms are happening more frequently and for longer periods of time.

It's why cultivating resilience is part of the modern seller's toolkit. Resilience helps us to bounce back from setbacks and even use them as a springboard for future success. It's knowing that obstacles and challenges are part of the journey. The more resilience we have, the better we get at moving fluidly through them. I believe resilience is something we can actively build.

How to Practice as a Modern Seller

Commit to an energy routine. Next time you're on a flight, and you hear the flight attendant run through all the safety features of the metal tube you're sitting in, I hope you remember this section. He says that should oxygen be needed, that four oxygen masks will drop down from the compartment above you. The next instruction is to put the oxygen mask on yourself first, before you assist others. Why? Because you can't help anyone else when you don't have your own oxygen.

An energy routine is your form of sales oxygen. It's what will keep you performing better than your competition, serving your clients well and being able to bounce back in any situation. Everyone around you, including your customers, picks up on your level of vitality, and it makes a difference to selling success.

I had a conversation with a leader who shared with me that the first two hours of her day were compete chaos. It was full speed ahead the minute her eyes opened in the morning—getting her family ready and out the door, getting herself ready and out the door. Her daily planning was the window of time she spent driving in rush hour traffic, in between bites of a bagel and high-test coffee. She was fried before even walking into the office, which is not conducive to the sales activities and client meetings she had to be "on" for that day.

In the moments of our conversation, she realized that her energy routine was the culprit and needed an overhaul. She needed more oxygen. For her, that meant taking 15 minutes the night before to plan her next day, and waking up 45 minutes earlier than the rest of the house to focus on herself. Small tweaks can make a significant difference to your energy results.

An energy routine is physical, mental and even spiritual. It includes things like your fitness habits, sleep habits, nutrition, mental inputs and even how you operate in the first hour or two of your day. The key is to experiment and design an energy routine that works for you. And, know that what works for you today will evolve over time.

Reframe setbacks. When we're in a negative situation, it can be tough to pinpoint what to do next to make our way out of it. Especially a setback situation—a lost deal, an angry client, a sales presentation that didn't go well, or a sales slump. If you've been in sales for any amount of time, these things are absolutely going to happen. It's all in how we respond—learning from our mistakes and moving forward.

When I'm in the middle of a setback, I can easily forget that. I get so focused on what's going wrong and not on what's going right or what I can learn from it. One perspective is to reframe setbacks on a continuum, looking at them as temporary events that are part of the bigger picture. It's a perspective that helps to even out the natural highs and lows of modern selling. A setback doesn't mean we're a failure and it isn't the lowest of the low—but rather it becomes a point along the journey. When I find myself here I'll often journal on a few questions:

- What is one simple thing I can do today to make positive progress out of this setback?
- Will this setback matter in a year's time? In five years' time?
- What is this setback trying to teach me?
- What do I need to do to either avoid it altogether next time, or shorten the setback curve if it happens again?

Develop a gratitude practice. We live in a world of constantly questing for the next thing. Once we've achieved something, it's off to the races to better it. One of my strengths is the ability to be futuristic—seeing several steps ahead and painting a vision for what the future can be. This is very helpful for working with clients in problem solving, envisioning future states, idea generation, and innovation.

The shadow side of that skill is that I can easily gloss over the present. When this happens, I dismiss what's great about today, and the great things that are happening right now. Glossing over today puts me in this perpetual "future state," where I'm not appreciating the joys of the present and I'm always ruminating on what's next.

I've also heard it described as the gap, the space between where we are today and where we want to be.

Writing this book is a great example of the gap. I'm here today writing one section, knowing that there is much more on this journey before (and after) the book is your hands. Today's writing is one step to closing the gap. With that I have a choice: view the gap as a liability, something to be anxious about; or see it with a sense of gratitude—that I've made a lot of steps on the journey so far, and that with each writing session, I'm getting closer to closing the gap.

If we're growing as modern sellers, there will always be a gap. There's a balance between accepting that gap, while working toward closing it. When we close one gap, another gap will naturally present itself as the next progression. The balance comes in the form of a gratitude practice. I keep a journal on my nightstand; every evening I write down three things I'm grateful for (personal or professional) and one thing I've learned for the day.

I've filled lots of journals in this way and from time to time, I read through them. Usually, there are some themes that appear. I'm most grateful for the times I've stretched myself, the time I've invested with family and friends, focusing on my priorities or the time I've invested in something that has impacted someone else. These are all things worth reflecting on as modern sellers.

Another take on the gratitude practice is a success practice. At the end of each business day, capture three successes for the day that have helped you elevate your territory or your business growth.

Play out the worst-case scenario. I was introduced to this idea from the *Four Hour Workweek* by Tim Ferriss. Whatever the situation is you're faced with—a client situation, internal situation, or maybe you're considering a change of some kind—you can use this exercise. Our brains are hard-wired for protection, and we tend to immerse ourselves in what can go wrong and not what can go right. So, indulge your brain's protective side for a bit, and write down everything that can go wrong with that situation. This is your opportunity to get creative! Our brains can weave some outrageously creative stories and worst-case scenarios, 99.9 percent of which will never happen.

Once you've gotten it out of your system, ask yourself what would happen if that scenario actually came to pass. Would it maybe cause some discomfort that you need to work your way through? Would you survive? Would you figure it out? Would you be kicking yourself later if you didn't take the risk?

The worst-case scenario game plays on fear. When we make decisions from fear, we're usually making choices that only take into consideration the downside, and we lose our resilience. When we get those fears out of our heads and onto paper, they often lose their scariness. Modern sellers live at the edge of discomfort. They seek it out because that's where the growth opportunity is.

Get an outside perspective. One of my coaches, Jane Atkinson of The Wealthy Speaker, has a saying that applies perfectly to outside perspective. She says, "You can't see the label when you're inside the jar." She's used it with me more than once! We can get into our own heads, our own challenges, and get stuck inside of our jars, so to speak. We lose perspective and aren't able to accept or process new ideas.

Successful people (and modern sellers) get outside perspective. Period. They have a coach, a mentor or an adviser. They have their kitchen cabinet, those supportive people who will tell it like it is while remaining in their corner no matter what. If you don't have these people in your life, it's time to get them. I highly encourage you to create a formal coaching relationship with an expert—whether it's in the personal or professional realm. I've invested in specific coaches for selling skills, entrepreneurial skills and elevating my speaking practice. The investment into a coaching relationship will be a game changer for you as a modern seller—and if your organization doesn't pay for it, find a way to personally invest in it.

How to Practice as a Modern Sales Leader

Look for the signs of burnout in your team. The earlier you can pinpoint the telltale signs of burnout, the better odds you have of preventing future performance problems or even losing a rock star seller. Look for signs in your team members like: routinely working late nights and long weekends; those who are normally optimistic beginning to exhibit chronic negativity; or those who are normally high performers not turning in their usual results. It may be a blip on the radar, or it may be something more significant. Also, don't hesitate to lead the way for your team by making the prevention of burnout part of the conversation.

Reframe your coaching conversations. You play the role of coach to each of your team members; it's what you signed up for as a sales leader. The metrics are important—conversations on pipeline, opportunities, wins, losses and the like. And, this is the natural place we all go to in coaching conversations.

It's equally important that you're framing your conversations holistically, and including discussions around how your team members are managing themselves. What are they learning? What are they doing to show up at their best every day? What setbacks are they dealing with and how can you help them bounce back? What successes are they having? How can these be shared with other team members to help them grow as well?

KEY TAKEAWAYS

- To be a differentiator for your clients and their organizations, there should be a focus on YOU in the selling ecosystem.
- Your professional skills are one part of the ecosystem, but there's more to it. How you care for yourself, how you invest your time and how you prioritize your days, when combined with your professional skills, will make you unstoppable as a modern seller.
- Time is your most precious asset as a modern seller.
- Holistic approaches will help you create stronger client relationships, elevate your executive presence and put you on the direct path to productivity and results.
- Modern sellers are extremely selective with how they invest their time. They have fewer, but more significant goals. They're focused on high-quality priorities and actively work to avoid the urgent things passing themselves off as priorities.
- The typical to-do list needs a makeover. Because modern sellers are leaders (regardless of title), they work from a different set of lists to set them apart in the eyes of their customers and their organizations.
- Your level of resilience directly affects your sales results. Resilience practices like energy routines, reframing setbacks and heading off burnout will help you operate at the highest levels without losing yourself in the process.

IV.

THE MODERN SELLER IS **SOCIAL**

CHAPTER 10

The 3 R's and Turning Points

There are three things that we take with us no matter where we go in life: our results, our reputation, and our relationships. They're completely transferrable from one situation or experience to the next, and they build on one another. Out of these three, relationships are the foundation. Every relationship experience helps us learn and gives us a new perspective. This, in turn, helps us better connect in the next relationship.

I can trace nearly anything significant that has happened in my life to the power of strategic relationships—their connectivity, and their give and take. There have been two turning points in my sales career that drive home the value of strategic relationships and the social skillset.

The opportunity to build my career at IBM started with a strategic relationship that began with my very first inside sales role and continues to this day. The backstory is that I'd taken a career detour from that inside sales role, jumping into a very different opportunity I thought I would love. An IT consulting firm came calling and I became a consultant, working onsite at clients designing and developing custom database applications. I quickly realized that the role didn't fit me. At. All. The work wasn't inspiring, and I was living in a cubicle all day without much client contact.

After about six months, I knew my heart wasn't in it and I needed to course correct. In looking back, I know I would've eventually been fired from that job had this strategic relationship not intervened.

A connection I made while in that first inside sales role worked for IBM. There was an opening he thought I might be interested in, and he let me know about it. This checked many of my boxes: it was an opportunity to get back into sales in a client-facing role, and a chance to grow my career at one of the best companies in the world.

This connection became a strategic relationship because not only did he get my resume to right people, he introduced me to the hiring manager (his boss) and coached me on interviewing. He gave me advice on how to successfully land the role. This went way beyond what I was expecting, and in the end, I got the job. It was one of those experiences I can look back on and say changed my life.

The other turning point was when I left the relative safety of that sales role, stepping out to become an entrepreneur.

This was a big pivot, moving into a different industry—the training space. As an employee turned entrepreneur, there was a light-bulb moment where I realized I had a big problem: I had one project to start this fledging company. Apart from that, as well as a couple of connections in this new industry, I knew almost no one else. More importantly, no one knew me.

I remember the panic setting in. Maybe I'd made a huge mistake, and the best thing to do would be to turn back and return to what I knew. Until that point, my relationship ecosystems had been primarily within my sales territory and the four walls of the company where I worked. Now there was no longer a neat little box to fit into, with defined relationships and a defined sales identity. The challenge ahead would be building entirely new relationships and, as I would learn, building them much broader, deeper, and higher than I've ever done. I was also going to learn how to translate those initial relationships into closing sales and leading a successful business.

I'm happy to say I didn't give in to the panic or turn back. Instead, I decided I would rather try to build a business, even one that failed, then to look back in 10 years and say "shoulda, woulda, coulda." I decided to become a student of building relationships. Now, they have become the fuel for my selling success, and the fuel for reaching back and helping others succeed. Along the way, there are numerous strategies I've learned, created, failed at until I got it right, and still practice—all of which help me build relationships and sell in the modern world.

Why It Matters

So why does the social dimension matter in modern selling? It comes down to four basic principles:

1. **Buying decisions are increasingly being made by committee and consensus.** I wouldn't go so far as to say the single decision-maker scenario is dead because I've still experienced it, even in complex sales. It's just becoming less common. A growing reality is that more decisions require consensus building, whether overtly or behind the scenes. In RFP (request-for-proposal) situations, decisions are made by committees which represent multiple business units and stakeholders across the client.

In research conducted by CEB, the average number of decision makers in any given deal is 6.8, and the variety of those decision-making roles is becoming more complex across job function and geography. This means for you that there's a good chance of a buying role (and potential decision maker) where the relationship is weak. Sellers now must go wider and deeper in their relationship-building efforts, expanding beyond the usual departments in which they do business and stretching further into the organization.

2. You can make fewer cold calls. Someone recently asked me if selling has become tougher or easier in the last 10 years. In many ways, it's tougher (consensus decision making, as an example, or any of the other challenges I mentioned in earlier sections), but there's one key way it has become easier: Today's social platforms provide more access than ever before to reach people. We're just a connection or two away from decision makers or other influencers.

But, that means a lot of other people are as well. The noise has amplified. And, because we're all so connected through technology, those of us that build and maintain strong networks have the advantage. With strong networks, we can rise above the noise. Our ability to connect broadly and deeply can mean fewer cold calls. With fewer cold connections, you can gain access more quickly and with more support, because the beginning of a relationship has already been established through your network.

3. Selling is still about connecting to other human beings in a way that's genuine and adds value. In an age of artificial intelligence, machine learning, and predictive analytics, you still need to know how to connect with others at an emotional level.

In complex sales, technology isn't going to win or expand the business—you are, as a modern seller. To move up the value chain with your clients, relationship building isn't something you can delegate. Yes, you can leverage AI and machine learning technologies to accelerate pattern-finding and decision-making. But it's your relationship-building efforts that will produce the best results.

4. It expands your network ecosystems, which increases your reach and influence. I was first introduced to the concept of "ecosystems" by entrepreneur and author Judy Robinett in her book *How to Be a Power Connector.* My earlier story about stepping into entrepreneurship underscores Robinett's points, as my reach and influence were limited to my immediate world. At the time, my network ecosystem was small. By becoming an entrepreneur, I faced having to expand—not just the number of relationships, but also the level at which I was operating. I had to exercise my "growth mindset," to borrow a phrase from researcher Carol Dweck. I needed to build relationships with those who also valued their networks, could open doors for me, and I could do the same for them. This would allow me to amplify my own reach and influence. You're likely facing this too, especially if you're starting up a territory or market segment, moving into a new role, or you're realizing that to reach your quota objectives you must expand your reach and influence.

What It Looks Like

Here are a few examples of what social looks like in modern selling:

- **Board service for a non-profit or industry organization.** This experience can connect us to peers, industry leaders, strategic partnerships, and potential decision makers. I recently served on a board with an executive who worked for one of my key clients, but in a different business unit. I was doing business within one area of the company, and she offered to introduce me to a potential decision maker within another business unit. Without our common connection through board service, I likely wouldn't have had that opportunity for a trusted and direct introduction.

- **Fluidly moving a relationship from virtual to voice, from voice to in-person—and creating value each time.** One of my biggest client relationships had its beginnings in LinkedIn. In my case, it was a series of InMail messages via LinkedIn which led to an introductory phone call. How I structured that introductory phone call created the initial trust that eventually led to in-person conversations. The in-person conversations and further trust-building ultimately led to opportunities to bid on a single project. The delivery of that single project built even more trust and led to more projects, and then referrals to other clients in that decision maker's network. Everything connects.

- **The account leader with a target client, but no direct access.** He has decided to take a mixed prospecting approach to get some momentum. This includes finding at least three to five potential decision makers or influencers from the prospect on LinkedIn. Then he'll research his network for any intersection points, identifying where these connections could be warmed up with either more information or an introduction. There's also an upcoming event his company is sponsoring; he's partnering with his marketing team to send out targeted whitepapers and event invitations. By doing this, he'll know through his sales enablement platform if those have emails achieved successful open rates. The account leader can then follow up with phone calls.

IV.

THE MODERN SELLER IS **SOCIAL**

CHAPTER 11

The Social Framework: Strategies to Build Social Selling Capital

To develop the social dimension, it helps to have a little background on social capital. Social capital has its roots in sociology, but has made its way into business environments over the past few decades. Social capital is the collective value of our relationships and what is created through those relationships. The wider and deeper we invest in building relationships, the more social capital we create. The more social capital we create, the more valuable the goals we're able to reach.

A byproduct of social capital is momentum. Modern sellers get this. They have momentum because they're constantly focused on creating and leveraging their social capital. This momentum creates more qualified and valuable opportunities, and it puts them on a completely different level. Decision makers and other influencers look at them and interact with them differently because they know it's a relationship of deeper value.

Another way to think of social capital in everyday terms is like a bank account. Any healthy bank account has deposits and debits. We need them both equally, as one creates value and the other extracts value for something we need. Over time, the value of the account should continue to grow.

What are examples of these deposits or debits? I've heard them best described as the four T's: time, talent, treasure, and ties. They're assets we either have or we can develop to create value for ourselves and others.

Time: Our most precious non-renewable resource. Where, on what, and with whom we decide to invest our time creates the sum total of our success.

Talent: Our unique knowledge, skills, and experience that we can use to create forward progress on an idea, a problem, or an opportunity.

Treasure: Leveraging financial means to invest and accelerate growth in ourselves, in others, and in organizations.

Ties: The depth and breadth of our networks used to create connections among people, resources, and opportunities.

If time, talent, treasure, and ties are our assets, what's the currency on which those assets are traded? They are trust, generosity, and leverage. Combined, they open more doors, create more opportunities, and ultimately generate higher overall lifetime value in any relationships we create.

Trust

Trust is transparency and creates a sense of safety and vulnerability. Trust is finding alignment by openly sharing goals and values. It's sharing successes and struggles. It's knowing that intentions are true and commitments matter.

For example, I have a coach who is a fellow entrepreneur and selling expert who really lives by this concept. By our second conversation, he very openly shared what he most valued personally and professionally. And as someone who has built and sold several multi-million-dollar businesses, it wasn't the accolades he mentioned. Instead, he shared his struggles, shining a light on the stuff which doesn't get written about when you're receiving an award.

Right away that got my barriers down and my trust up. I became way more willing to do the same. It paved the way to a meaningful relationship more quickly, and it accelerated my ability to solve what I had hired him to help me with. Strategic relationship builders are able to build trust quickly, and continue to earn it for the life of the relationship.

Generosity

I first heard this concept from Keith Ferrazzi, author of *Never Eat Alone*. He calls generosity the fuel of our networks. Generosity means that when we've decided to invest in a relationship, we give of our time, talent, treasure, and ties with no strings attached. We give from a place of genuinely wanting to create something better for those we're building strategic relationships with. Without generosity, we risk our relationships becoming focused on keeping score because we have an expectation of getting something in return. This prevents us from investing more deeply into them. But, when we build relationships with others who also live from a place of generosity, the returns will arrive. This provides the opportunity to earn more business while also creating longer-term value.

Leverage

Simply put, it's the ask. Leverage is a willingness to ask for what's needed to move something forward. It's also offering something to someone in your strategic network—usually one the four Ts. This could be a micro-commitment (typically something of lower value given early in a relationship to continue to building trust) or a macro-commitment (something of larger value, generally in a more established relationship with a longer history of trust).

In the context of modern selling, leverage is also what helps us to close business. We often make closing business much more complicated and awkward than it needs to be. The sales process is a way to provide and ask for the appropriate level of commitments from our prospects. This is a natural and genuine way of using leverage.

Going back to the bank account analogy, an essential element of this is the balance: the balance of the overall account and the give and take of the relationship. If the give and take gets out of balance, that usually means one person is investing more in the relationship than the other. That's why the credits and debits are equally important. For a strategic relationship to be successful, everyone involved needs a sense of giving (deposits) and receiving (debits).

The Social Framework

Everything in my work and in selling comes down to my strategic network—the relationships I build, how I add value to those relationships, and how those relationships when leveraged in the right way, create even more collective value. I'm still a work in progress, a student. And, as any good student would do, I'm always looking for strategies I could use or steps that I could take to help me get better.

From this, my own framework started to emerge; one to help me with all the components of relationship building. There are four elements to the Social Framework: Mindset, Goals, Network Ecosystem, and Habits. This framework will help you build your own overall network and identify strategic relationships you will need to invest in to reach your goals.

Mindset

Having the mindset of a strategic relationship builder is the foundational element of the framework. Without this, it's challenging to make the other elements of the framework work. You must truly believe—and internalize—that you are a strategic relationship builder and tap into the 4 Ts you currently have. Depending on where you are in your career, you'll have more of some than others. The first step toward success is recognizing that you have everything within you to build powerful relationships with peers, internal leaders, centers of influence, prospects, C-level decision makers, and industry thought leaders. It all comes down to your decision to choose to see yourself in that way, and treat relationship building as one of the most important things you do every day.

The lightbulb moment for me was understanding that I needed to work on the other elements of the framework *while* building the mindset component. When we're learning new things the mindset typically isn't there yet. The decision to take uncomfortable action comes first and implementing the rest of the framework continues to build the mindset and motivation.

There are five key elements of mindset which separate the most influential relationship builders from everyone else. We covered two of them a little earlier, trust and generosity. Here are the other three:

Leadership Identity: When leading programs on social capital, one of the first exercises I take attendees through is on leadership identity. I ask people to identify an influential leader in their life and write down specifically what that person did to build a relationship with them. Many people cite parents, teachers, coaches, work leaders, or even a peer in the room. These are some of the responses I usually receive:

- That person challenged my thinking
- They showed interest in my perspectives
- They gave effective and kind feedback
- They shared their knowledge and resources
- They created opportunities for me
- They helped me solve my biggest challenges

I'll then ask them to describe the overall relationship by completing the sentence: "It is/was a relationship that inspired _____." Answers to this usually include:

- Trust
- Psychological safety
- Challenge
- Growth
- Continuous learning
- Engagement

Wouldn't we love our prospects and clients to say these things about us? Wouldn't it be great if they identified you as an influential leader who helped them? Leadership, social capital, and selling are intertwined. Effective sellers are leaders who understand the value of social capital and the importance of developing relationships. The quality of our leadership influences the quality of our relationships and sales results. Every challenge our decision makers grapple with requires sellers to show up as leaders.

I'd encourage you to do this exercise for yourself or with your sales teams. The best sellers are leaders who decide how they want to show up in the world. They choose their leadership identity. And they know to achieve meaningful goals they need to build social capital from a leadership perspective.

Intent: The best relationship builders are intentional. They're purposeful in choosing the relationships they build, and in discerning which relationships get more of their valuable time and attention. They're able to be intentional because they take the time upfront to understand the other person's goals and values.

When they know these important pieces of information, they can add the right level of value at the right time and continue to cultivate the relationship.

Hand in hand with intent, great relationship builders approach strategic relationships as team-building exercises. Rather than look at it as "what's in it for me," or "what's in it for you," the relationships become "what's in it for us and what can we create together?" Great relationship builders continuously learn how to improve the value they bring to the relationship. This can only happen when there is a trust that together we are creating a result or outcome. This team-building intent works for any relationship or situation: prospects who don't know you well yet, big complex RFP situations, or existing clients where you're looking to expand the relationship.

Lifetime Value: When I ask the question, "What holds you back from building strategic relationships?" the answers are usually universal, regardless of the audience (even sales audiences). Things like:

- No time—falls off the priority list when urgent things come up
- Not comfortable
- Feels like I'm taking advantage of others
- Not sure exactly how—I need a process
- I don't want to be responsible for the outcomes; I don't want to look bad

The antidote to these triggers is a lifetime value approach to relationships. In modern selling, our approach to relationships and decisions can't be defined by that first deal or the opportunity that's right in front of us. It can't be defined by "what can you do for me right now." When we think only about the present moment rather than the long tail of the relationship, we get stuck in a "me only" mentality. This thinking sucks us into the mental barriers that keep us from building important strategic relationships. It also puts us at risk of losing focus on our intent and damaging the trust in that relationship.

To take a lifetime value lens for every relationship, whether it's with a center of influence, a prospect, an RFP decision committee, or an existing client, ask yourself:

- Am I making the right level of effort?
- Have I added more value than what I'm asking for?
- Will this action continue to positively build the relationship for the long term?

Goal Setting

The second part of the Social Framework is goal setting. In our sales roles, the biggest goal we're usually working toward is our quota goal. It's an external goal set for us by our leadership teams. Our work then becomes creating the opportunities and closing the business which gets us to the goal. But within the quota attainment goal, modern sellers know the value of setting social goals.

Social goals are accomplished through strategic relationships. By using that lens, goals around selling become less about us and more about being of service, looking for ways to contribute in every selling or client situation. It's the realization that any significant goal requires relationships—and significant goals separate modern sellers from average sellers. Through this approach, modern sellers not only achieve this year's quota, they also create an environment where they have momentum for the long-term.

As you think about your territory, your business or your role, ask yourself what goals are meaningful. I encourage you to complete the visioning exercise outlined in the Entrepreneurial dimension of the book. I also encourage reflection on professional goals, selling goals, and personal goals. When we're building a vision or pursuing a goal that stretches us, it doesn't become just about professional success; it's also personal because we change in the process.

When I lead this type of work with sales organizations, I ask them to start by creating their territory vision. This gets them into the mindset as entrepreneurs and owners of their respective territories. With their vision as their guide, they then decide on the most meaningful goals they need in the next one to three years to accomplish the vision. Usually, those goals become much bigger because they start to see how the goals will make the vision happen.

Below are several goals coming from this work, to spark your thinking as you create your vision and individual goals:

- Develop a new vertical market
- Increase my presence within my industry
- Create a community that brings together clients, prospects, and industry leaders
- Expand into a customer set my competition has dominated
- Seek out new partnerships to expand my reach and create new opportunities
- Build a skill needed for a pivot, and create opportunities in the new area
- Launch a new product or service

The most important ingredient I've found to help me with goal setting is to dig into my motivation, and significance behind it.

Without an internal motivation it's easy to get lost. I've set plenty of goals I've fallen short on or decided to quit because my internal motivation wasn't strong enough to keep me going. In sales environments, motivation often defaults to external performance metrics. As sellers, we're recognized and rewarded for achieving quota and for winning. Becoming a modern seller doesn't mean that goes away, but it does mean integrating and balancing the short and long term. Social goals can help us deliver on performance goals with integrity and help us keep our focus on building our business or territory for the long term.

Here are some questions to consider while building out your goals:

- Why is this goal significant to me, my clients, and my organization?
- Does this goal support the vision I set out for my business or territory?
- Do I want this goal with my head (does it make sense to pursue), and with my heart (am I passionate about it)?
- Is this a short-term goal (within this year), or a long-term goal (12-plus months)? How does this affect my decision to pursue the goal?
- How will this goal change my business or territory?
- How do I see myself evolving as a modern seller and leader because of pursuing this goal?
- What resources do I need to begin creating movement toward this goal?
- What would happen if this goal isn't realized? What might get in the way of making this goal happen?

Here's an example of this goal-setting approach from my sales life:

Goal: One of my aspirational goals is to expand keynote speaking within my existing business, as a mainstage keynoter on sales and leadership. It becomes a revenue stream of its own and a lead generator for the sales and leadership development programs my company offers.

Significance: This goal matters because it will give me the opportunity to connect and share my message with larger audiences. It's a larger platform for the work I'm passionate about, which is developing modern sellers and leaders. It's pushing me out of what's comfortable. It's significant to my organization because it will create new revenue streams, new employee opportunities, and new opportunities for high-value client work.

Here's an example from another modern seller:

Goal: One of my goals is to help the company grow into an entirely new business segment. We've been a key player in our existing segments and we've maxed out on our growth opportunities. This new segment is untapped (also untapped by our competitors) with lots of room for growth. My vision is to be the leading expert in this new market. So, the goals are to build the market and get initial growth going. From there, I'd like to potentially build and lead the sales teams that will continue to grow it from there.

Significance: This goal matters to my company because it will create opportunity for our employees, and it will create opportunities to grow beyond our current constraints. It represents a legacy for our current CEO, and for me it's a new challenge. I especially like the possibility of building and leading teams.

Use these ideas to create goals that matter to you. Social goals involve building and leveraging relationships, in the service of our visions as business leaders.

Network Ecosystems and the Social Relationship Formula

Your network ecosystem is where your relationships live. Your network ecosystem helps you identify the relationships you'll need, evaluate their current strength, and systematize your efforts.

Before we get into the network ecosystem and mapping, let's cover the Social Relationship Formula. I created the formula because I needed a way think tactically about the how of building and maintaining a relationship. It helps me to more easily evaluate the overall status of a relationship and how it fits into my network ecosystem.

$$(\text{Create} + \text{Sustain})^2 - \text{Leverage} = \text{Social Capital}$$

To break down the elements of this formula:

Create: This is the early stage of a relationship, or it may also be a relationship that isn't yet built. Examples of this include research on new contacts, an introduction at a networking event, or the touchpoints you're planning for a prospect. This could also be a relationship re-connection—think of relationships in your network which may have gone dormant and that you may need to rekindle based on your goals.

The common thread among these scenarios is they're all early stage, where the primary goals are to establish connection and trust. It's where you continue to learn about the relationship—what the other person values and what their goals are—and how that information aligns with your goals and values.

How long does this phase take? It depends on how quickly you can figure out how their goals and values align with yours, and how fast you're able to build trust. I can identify relationships where within one conversation I knew I wanted to take the relationship to the next level—Sustain. In those cases, it was easy to achieve initial value exchanges—ideas, sending an article, or even making an introduction. In other early-stage relationships where the trust never materialized, the relationship didn't make it out of this stage.

Sustain: This is where a decision is made to go deeper into developing the relationship. Early-stage trust is strong, and each person is willing to make more investment into growing it. If you noticed the squared part of the formula, it's a reminder to put twice as much effort into creating and sustaining relationships as we do into leveraging them.

Because it takes consistent commitment over time to keep trust high, the Sustain stage is also where you determine how much long-term effort to invest in the relationship. You begin to sense the balance of the relationship, and how the other person views its overall value: are each of you putting in about the same amount of effort, or is something lopsided?

When the effort is balanced, there are equal exchanges of value, trust remains high, and there's a shared desire to keep the relationship's momentum. If one person is over-contributing and the other under-contributing, the account balance becomes out sync, trust can drop, and it can stall any progress of working toward a common goal. Not all relationships require—nor should they get—your valuable time, energy, and attention.

Leverage: To leverage a relationship is to master the ask. The level of the ask depends on a few factors, such as the degree of trust in the relationship, whether it's the right person or situation, and whether the value is there.

Some valuable lessons I've learned along the way when it comes to leverage:

- **Others want to offer value.** Asks allow the other person the opportunity to be of service. When trust and sustainability are high, it's a natural progression.

- **It's just as important to proactively offer my help as it is to ask.** When I see something that may help someone in my network I offer it up. When I take this extra step, it does two things: it further solidifies the relationship and builds my confidence in making asks.

- **The level of risk is in the eye of the beholder.** Don't pre-judge the ask. What may be a big ask to you may not be a big ask to someone else.

As I was writing this book, I made a list of the endorsements I wanted to include. There was a very well-known author and thought leader in the sales world on that list. We had a built a strong relationship over the years, sharing ideas and information. I had introduced her to one of my clients several years ago, which resulted in business for both of us. The Create and Sustain parts of the relationship were all there.

Even with that, I was still nervous about the ask. I happened to be in her hometown for a conference and scheduled a breakfast with her to reconnect. I wanted to make sure I didn't leave that meeting without making the ask. I had built it up in my mind as something big, something she would need to think about.

But an interesting thing happened when I made the ask: The entire exchange took about 30 seconds. I received an immediate "yes." She was flattered (and surprised) I would make the effort to see her in person to make the ask.

Create Your Network Ecosystem Map

Using one of your own goals and the Social Relationship Formula, you can build out your network ecosystem map. Do this in any format that works best for your learning style—paper or digital, lists or visual mind maps. When it's in a format you can systematize and use weekly, it can become a habit. If you have a CRM capable of accommodating it, all the better because it can then be used in conjunction with other selling activities and tracking methods. To create your network ecosystem map:

Brainstorm the relationship roles you think you'll need to accomplish the goal. Right now, you don't need names next to those roles, just the roles themselves. Using my goal of building a keynote speaking revenue stream, my list might look like this:

- Skill coaches
- Corporate event planners
- Speaker bureaus

- Current clients
- New clients and prospects
- Peers in sales roles and sales leadership roles
- Industry associations
- Peer speakers at my current level
- Speakers who have done this successfully
- Vendor relationships

Put some names to these roles. Begin filling in names for these roles you've identified. I find it valuable to get help from a trusted advisor that can relate to my goal. It increases the creativity and quality of potential relationships I can build. You'll want to add as much information as you have, like contact information, context on the relationship, or other data helpful to you. Later you'll prioritize your list and approach based on relationship strength.

Note whether the people are internal or external. Label the relationship as internal or external to your organization. You'll need both types of relationships to achieve your social goals. This exercise is valuable because you can quickly see where you might have internal or external gaps. In our example of the sales professional who is building a new market segment, chances are good he will need to build just as many—if not more—internal relationships as external client-facing or partner relationships.

Determine the relationship type. In their *Harvard Business Review* article "How Leaders Create and Use Networks," authors Herminia Ibarra and Mark Lee Hunter describe three types of relationships our network ecosystems need: Operational, Personal, and Strategic. These are the relationship types a modern seller needs to pursue bigger goals. Categorizing them in this way provides insight as to the *level* at which you're operating:

- An Operational relationship is one related to your role and likely has functional expertise. It brings "depth" in terms of the working relationship. In my example, peer speakers and my vendor relationships could fall into this category.
- A Personal relationship is one which helps you "enhance your development." It provides "breadth" because it is often external and connected to other network ecosystems where you may not have access. My executive coach, speaking coach, and professional associations fill this role for me.
- A Strategic relationship is one which will help you with business direction and big-picture thinking. It may even include stakeholders in your goal. These relationships bring "leverage" because they have internal and external connections and may be able to connect you upwards. In my example, speaker bureaus, centers of influence, and current clients are strategic relationships to help me reach my goal.

Evaluate the relationship strength. This is where the Social Relationship Formula will help you to evaluate the strength of your relationship. Ask the following questions:

- Are you at the beginning stages or need to renew the connection? If so, you're in Create mode.
- Are you at the beginning stages of Sustain? You may need to add more value depending on what potential ask you could want to make in the future.

- Have you added enough value so you're at a point where you can leverage the relationship? You may be ready to test it out with a smaller-risk ask, or you may know that the relationship has a very strong account balance and feel confident leveraging it. Here's how I classify relationship strength:
  - ++ (Strong Leverage potential)
  - + (Strong Sustain; may need more value for Leverage)
  - O (Neutral; might still be in Create or early Sustain phase)
  - - (Very early Create or Renewal stage)

Systematize with a dashboard. Just like our CRMs have us log our sales activity, you'll want to log your relationship activity. If your CRM becomes your core dashboard, you should be able to add your notes directly into a contact. Your CRM may also allow you to treat this as a separate opportunity or initiative with relationship tasks; this approach can help you track at a big-picture level and gauge your relationship-building progress against your goal. I've found a dashboard approach keeps me focused as relationships grow and more opportunities occur.

This process of mapping and evaluating relationships, centered around a significant goal, helps us to see patterns. Patterns reveal where we have relationship strengths and opportunities. It can also help better prioritize where to invest time and build social capital.

With your network ecosystem map, you can further analyze it by asking yourself these questions:

- **Where am I strong?** For example, do I have a good mix of operational, personal and strategic relationships? How balanced is my mix of internal and external relationships? Do I have enough relationships where I've added significant value to potentially leverage them for my goal?

- **Where are the relationship gaps?** Either there is no relationship today or there is a relationship where I can and should be providing more value.
- **Where can I stretch?** The stretch often shows up as a relationship gap because we tend to build relationships where we're most comfortable. Modern sellers look to build the relationships that will stretch them because those relationships will accelerate them toward their goals.
- **Where can I pay it forward?** These are relationships where you can be additive, but there's likely not an opportunity for leverage. Examples here might be mentoring or volunteering. They add to your network ecosystem but may not play a direct role in accomplishing your goal.

Internal/ External (I/E)	**Relationship Type** (Operational, Personal, Strategic)	**Relationship Strength** ++ (Leverage) + (Sustain/Leverage) O (Create/Sustain) -- (Create)	**Notes** (Examples: Where can I add value to them? What do I need help with? How will this tie to my goal?)

Habits

So far, we've covered your mindset, social goals and network ecosystem map. The last piece of the Social Framework is your habits as a modern seller or sales leader.

As important as your other daily selling habits, your social habits are the small actions you're consistent with that further your strategic relationships. These habits have helped me to quickly accelerate my progress:

Connect with Centers of Influence regularly. Centers of influence (COIs) are those people in your network who are very well connected, both broadly and deeply. They could be operational, personal, or strategic. They understand the value in sharing their expertise and connections. They can also connect you with other COIs. When you've established who in your network are your COIs, and then those who are most aligned to your goals, those are relationships you'll want to devote your time and give your greatest focus.

Join an organization and the highest-profile committee that ties directly to your goal. If your network ecosystem contains industry organizations, target two which can most directly impact your goal. With two, choose one to join with the intention of membership only and the other in which you'll make a deeper social capital investment. Begin with the one that will get your greater focus, and then join their highest profile committee. This will help you immediately raise your profile, make connections more quickly, and provide value in a genuine way.

Connect people weekly. In every conversation I have with someone in my network, it's my intention to connect them to other people, to ideas, or with resources to help them reach their goals. Each week, I make it a goal to connect at least two people in my network with something of importance to them. With your network ecosystem map, this will provide more focus as you're working with a specific set of relationships and goals.

Develop strategic alliances. This one habit has helped me reach my goals more quickly and with greater impact. I've found it works best when you have similar goals, similar target markets, and complementary offerings. As you look at your goal, who in your network ecosystem might have a similar goal? Who might be looking to increase his or her impact at a level similar to you? Who offers products and services that complement you, and serves the same types of markets? Currently, I'm exploring a strategic partnership with a membership organization in the HR space that is building their speaker bureau and wants to offer sales training to their membership. Our sales training offerings complement their existing programs, and we serve many of the same types of clients. This strategic partnership represents a growth opportunity for both of us while also creating more value for our joint clients.

Develop an expertise you can become known for. In a world of increasing commoditization, modern sellers stand out with a specific expertise or niche. Does your current goal give you this opportunity? In my own modern selling journey, my goal became to evolve from a seller of hardware technology to an expert in mobile computing for education. If you're in an industry where this is particularly challenging, look at your approach, or *the how* behind what you do. How can you make the experience better? Can you differentiate in how you deliver your product or service? Your expertise or niche can become the *how* instead of the *what.*

Practice the art of the ask with higher-level relationships. There are going to be times when you need to make an ask to move a significant goal forward and you'll be lacking the right level of social capital. If your network ecosystem map has gap with strategic relationships or centers of influence, you'll need to add those to your mix. When I've needed a higher-level relationship where I need to build my social capital, I like to ask for advice and perspective. I learn from their expertise and begin to understand what's important to them so I can find ways to add value to the relationship. I'll share my goals, too, and they'll often be willing to help brainstorm ideas, or possibly provide sponsorship toward my goal at some future point.

Cultivate questions that connect. Questions are powerful. Whenever I connect with someone I have several ready, much like when I'm preparing discovery questions for a sales conversation. While questions for specific selling conversations may look a little different from network ecosystem conversations, I usually find some crossover between them. Below are a few of my questions based on Create, Sustain, and Leverage. These work just as well with your network ecosystem as they do with your sales conversations.

Create/Sustain Questions:

- "What is something you're working on right now that's exciting for you?"
- "What are some of the trends you're seeing in your industry?"
- "What is a goal you're working toward?"
- "How do you like to stay connected?"
- "What can I do to help you right now?" (This question comes from sales strategist and center of influence, Jen E. Miller. Its simplicity is unexpected, and it gets people thinking.)

Leverage Questions:

- "How would you suggest I go about...?"

- "Would you be willing to...?"
- "What's a next step I could take with ...?"
- "I appreciate your willingness to help. How can I pay it forward?"

Create a consistent and positive experience. Your conversations are your opportunity to create a positive and lasting impression—one which will lead to strong social capital. With bigger goals and higher-level COIs, stakeholders, and decision makers, your attention to these details are expected. If you're going to set the conversation, prioritize the time to prepare for it and lead it. Know your goals for the conversation, send out a short agenda ahead of time, and have your questions ready. Be prepared to lead the conversation, set any next action steps and follow through. These don't have to be overdone to be done right, and your preparation will set you apart.

Download and analyze your connections quarterly. With today's technology, we have connections and data in many places. These include LinkedIn, your CRM, your address books, your other social sites, and probably some spreadsheets—each contains the valuable data which comprises your network ecosystem. Prioritize your top locations where your connections are stored. Mine are LinkedIn, my CRM, and my digital address books. With some of these sources, you may have to request your data be sent to you; it becomes a good practice to request your data on a quarterly basis. I'll review my data sources, and based on my current goals, determine which connections I'd like to focus on within my network ecosystem.

KEY TAKEAWAYS

- Modern sellers build the social dimension for some key reasons: more decisions today are made by buying committees, which means that relationships must be wider and deeper than ever before. Modern sellers can make fewer cold calls because of their network ecosystem, and they have more reach and influence because of it.
- The social dimension is even *more valuable* in this age of artificial intelligence (AI). While AI provides valuable insights and can help us make better decisions with data—it's still about human connection.
- Social capital is the collective value of our relationships and what is created through those relationships. The more we invest, the more social capital we create. As our social capital grows we can reach goals more quickly and with greater impact.
- Time, talent, treasure, and ties increase your social capital and accelerate strategic relationship building.
- The Social Framework is your compass as a modern seller. The framework consists of your mindset, goals, network ecosystem, and habits.
- There are five key elements to mindset: leadership identity, intent, generosity, trust, and lifetime value.

KEY TAKEAWAYS

- For modern sellers, social goals go beyond quota attainment and into significance. It begins with your vision for your territory, and then developing one or two significant goals that will help accomplish your vision.
- Your network ecosystem is your most valuable asset. The strength, breadth, and depth of your network ecosystem will determine how quickly and how successfully you accomplish your most significant goals.
- There are several types of relationships in every healthy network ecosystem. Your network ecosystem map can help you to identify those relationships and determine where you have strengths and gaps. The Social Relationship Formula will help you to develop and leverage those relationships in a strategic and genuine way.
- Your habits are your daily actions that cultivate your network ecosystem. Just as you develop your daily sales actions, these are your daily relationship actions. They'll often have crossover because they directly support one another.

V.

THE MODERN SELLER IS AN **AMBASSADOR**

CHAPTER 12

The Bridge to Lifetime Customers

To create my vision of a modern seller and the most important dimensions needed for the new sales economy, I interviewed dozens of sales professionals and sales leaders. I mined my own experiences as a seller and entrepreneur. And, I researched the work of other sales and business experts.

As I was assembling patterns of skillsets, behaviors, failures, and successes, one word seemed to best describe these experts, sellers, and leaders. One word that also encompasses the other themes of agile, entrepreneurial, holistic, and social.

Ambassador.

These modern sellers were all ambassadors.

In a political and cultural sense, an ambassador is a bridge between two countries. A brand ambassador describes someone who's fiercely loyal to a company or product, and uses their influence to create buzz and followers for it.

What makes a modern seller an ambassador in the new sales economy? How do you know if you are one, or if you have them on your sales team? An ambassador is:

An **Owner.** This concept comes from my friend and corporate culture expert Greg Hawks (you can learn more about his work at www.hawksagency.com). After years of owning and renting properties, he discovered there are usually three distinct types of people living in his properties: owners, renters, and vandals.

Owners treated everything with a high-level of care; they took pride in and treated the property as if they owned it. Renters were the middle of the road – they cared for the property somewhat, but not at the level of an owner. And the vandals, they usually ended up ruining the property at some point. You can guess which was his favorite group of people to work with.

Ambassadors are owners. They hold themselves responsible and accountable for all aspects of the client or prospect relationship. They don't pass the buck, and they take pride in their ownership.

An **Expert.** Ambassadors proactively develop their expertise in an area or two, and it's what they become known for. They're open and willing to share that expertise—whether internally or externally. They're also humble, approachable, and curious. They'll dive into a topic they want to learn more about—and then share what they've learned with others around them.

You know an expert in two ways.

- People come to them for the knowledge they're known for.
- People still come to them, even for the knowledge they aren't known for, because they'll usually be able to point people in the right direction.

An **Elevator.** An ambassador creates lift, and they can elevate virtually any situation in which they find themselves. It might be offering a viewpoint that challenges a sales team in a problem-solving situation, asking *the* question that gets a prospect thinking differently, taking a leadership role in a pursuit, offering an optimistic word of encouragement, or providing thoughtful feedback. Ambassadors intentionally look for ways to elevate others and leave a situation better than they found it.

Impact-oriented. An ambassador looks to create impact—whether they initiate it, contribute to it, or support it. Creating positive impact—or avoiding negative impact—is what our customers and prospects are usually looking for in some way. Impact can also be internal; ambassadors aren't afraid to challenge the status quo inside their own organizations. Because they have proven themselves over time, they've earned the social capital and latitude to speak up. In these situations, an ambassador isn't viewed as simply a squeaky wheel, but as someone working to elevate the organization.

For example, one sales professional I interviewed challenged a long-standing contract his company had with a strategic partner. The existing contract was outdated, costing the company millions of dollars annually; competitors had recently negotiated better deals with this same partner. Because this sales rep was viewed as an ambassador, he was able to work with his internal teams to renegotiate the contract. The results not only benefited him. This new contract had a positive impact on margins for other sales teams, and in turn created a positive impact for the entire company.

Strategic and tactical. Ambassadors move fluidly between strategic thinking and tactical execution. (More on that in the Entrepreneurial dimension). They're equally comfortable talking high-level business strategy, and then pivoting into a conversation that gets tactical and helps figure out the *how* of realizing that strategy. They understand both languages, so they can help the strategists and the tacticians better understand one another. This ability to translate usually means that they can get to results more quickly, and with better outcomes.

A **Unifier.** Earlier in the agility dimension, I cover the value of strategic speed and research conducted by The Forum Corporation. Another element of strategic speed they uncovered that gets to better results more quickly is unity. Unity means we're all on the same page and moving in the same direction. Unity matters both internally, within our business units, and externally, with our clients and prospects. You know that person who seems to have a knack for getting internal buy-in and breaking down silos? The person who can get a decision maker or other influencer on board? They're your unifiers. Ambassadors are unifiers because they can envision the commonalities and acknowledge the differences. They're usually successful at getting everyone to yes, because they can find the mutual benefit.

A **Loyalty magnet.** Customer experience and client loyalty might be buzzwords but focusing on them pays off. A loyal customer or client creates much more value for us. In fact, the likelihood of selling to an existing loyal client is between 60 percent and 70 percent. The likelihood of selling to a new client is only five percent to 20 percent.

Ambassadors know a loyal client is one emotionally invested not only in their company, but in them as a person. Because of this, they focus on being loyalty magnets. They take the time to know and track what their clients expect from the relationship. They either directly own that experience themselves, or they build the right relationships internally to make sure their peers create that same level of loyalty.

A **Lifetime value creator.** Ambassadors balance the "win right now" and the "win for a lifetime" mindsets. The initial win is only the beginning of the relationship with a new client. The job becomes growing that relationship over time and keeping that client with you for the long term. Every interaction with a client is an opportunity to either increase (or unfortunately decrease) the overall lifetime value. I've seen (and experienced) many, many times the amount of effort—hours, money, expertise—that sales teams put into winning a new relationship, only to see the experience deteriorate after that initial win. Lifetime value goes both ways: it's the value we create for the client, but also what they can create for us, and what we can create together.

Their own brand. Ambassadors actively create their own brand in the marketplace. They don't rely on their company to create their brand for them. Their brand is one that aligns with their company and at the same time, also sets them apart. Ambassadors know their clients do business with them first, and their companies second. They're active in social channels, they treat their territory like a community, and they make a bigger effort to be visible. They're leaders, they're well known in their industry, and they create followers.

Why It Matters

Why does being an ambassador matter to modern selling? Or if I'm a sales leader, why do I need to create a team of ambassadors?

The new sales economy is evolving from transactional to connected.

The connected economy is a phrase attributed to marketing expert Seth Godin. Economic value has shifted over the decades from a single focus on transactions or the production of things, to today where relationships and connections are more crucial than ever before in creating value.

To see how this shift has played out, look at the *Fortune* 500. Created in 1955, companies that dominated the early list included General Motors, Exxon Mobil, Chrysler, and U.S. Steel. Flash forward to 2017, and while you still see companies like General Motors and Exxon Mobil, you also see companies like Google, Amazon, and Facebook. Companies that once dominated by producing things are now sharing the stage with companies that dominate by creating connections.

The balance to this viewpoint is remembering that in sales our primary goal is still to transact business—to move product or sell services. That doesn't go away. But what ambassadors do well is put things in the right order. They leverage the connected economy to move the right product, to sell the right services, to the right people. Ambassadors are the perfect bridge between connection and transaction.

The Amazon effect has reached B2B.

It used to be that B2B and B2C selling were different worlds. You either did one or the other, but never both. I grew up in B2B selling, and to be honest, those of us in B2B probably looked down just a bit on our B2C peers. Today, the tables have turned, and there's been a blending of the two worlds. In fact, B2B can take some lessons from B2C.

Our B2B clients now expect to apply their B2C experiences to their business worlds. They want their experiences with places like Amazon to be duplicated in even the most complex of situations. They want easy access to accurate information and comparison research. They want direct access to you and your company via social platforms. They want to gather their own peer reviews and social proof. They want to quickly get other recommendations. They want easy order, easy delivery, easy service, and easy return.

Easy in B2B, right?

"Satisfaction" is now the lowest common denominator.
Remember the days of customer satisfaction surveys, when the highest rating was "highly satisfied?" That was *the* bar. If you had a highly satisfied customer, you had arrived. Today, satisfaction is considered table stakes; it's an entry point instead of a destination. Instead, we need to focus on moving the needle toward loyalty, and even beyond that to create client ambassadors.

A Rain Group benchmark report noted this trend nearly 10 years ago in their 2009 *How Clients Buy* report on professional services. Even client respondents who would rate themselves as somewhat or even highly satisfied were anywhere from 52 percent to 72 percent likely to switch their providers.

No matter what product or service you sell, these figures should wake you up. Even if the numbers are different in your industry, the trend is probably similar. If you review your list of clients who you believed to be satisfied or even highly satisfied, and 52 percent of them could switch on you at any moment, what would that do to your sales results?

You'll reach a commoditization tipping point no matter how specialized or sophisticated your product or service.

During my days of selling personal computing products, I remember prospects and customers often viewing it as buying a commodity. The lowest price won. Even our peers in other divisions of the company saw it that way. But internally within our division, we did everything we could to position ourselves as solution providers and consultative sellers. It was a daily struggle to rise above the commodity label.

Today, I see even the most sophisticated of products and services fighting commoditization. Everything these days is available "as a service" or "as a subscription." That means that it can be easily turned off, stopped, or deleted at the click of the mouse or touch of the screen.

Fighting commoditization early in my sales career taught me that no one could commoditize me. It was up to me to be the differentiator. Even if I did sell a commodity product, how I operated could help me move from being viewed as a commodity to a specialty. While that wasn't a guarantee, it definitely gave me a level of control and creativity. The product was the product, but it was up to me to create an experience that would turn prospects into customers, and then move them along the loyalty path toward ambassadors.

What It Looks Like

Here are a few examples of what Ambassador sales approaches look like in daily sales life:

- A professional services consultant who leverages an initial win to begin a lifetime value journey. This was a small, competitive win for an initial project. The success of this project hinges on everyone on her team delivering in their role. Things like staying true to the initial scope, creating positive service touchpoints, and strong project deliverables are only the beginning. She sees a lot of possibilities beyond this project; creating value in this initial win will set her up for future opportunities.

- It's year end, and there's lots of pressure to bring in every deal. There's pressure to make it count—for your quota, your leader's quota, and reporting results to Wall Street. As an ambassador, you know dropping prices for the short-term or pressuring a customer to buy on your schedule weakens lifetime value. It will affect your reputation, the relationship, and bottom-line profitability.
- The sales professional who works with his big prospect to co-create solutions during the sales process. After some initial intelligence gathering and discovery have been done, this seller schedules idea-generation sessions. Rather than create potential solutions in a vacuum, this seller works with his prospects to brainstorm. Because he does this, his prospects have much more buy-in and advocate internally on his behalf.
- The seller who is publishing her own thought leadership pieces, via her own blog, her LinkedIn profile, and other social platforms. These pieces align with her company, but it also extends her own leadership brand. She's showcasing her unique expertise and point of view. She's generating more interaction with her content, increasing her followership and her social influence. She's setting herself apart from her peers in a noisy space.
- This same seller who's publishing her thought leadership and elevating her brand, is *also* able to use her content and role to more easily connect to her prospects and clients—in a non-salesy way. Because she takes an ambassador point of view, she sees herself as a connector. When she connects people within her prospect and client network to her work and other thought leaders, she's keeping herself from being commoditized.

- The sales professional who can easily move between strategic thinking and tactical application. In a complex sale, he can talk with his prospect about the big picture of *what* a solution could mean to solving a challenge, and then just as quickly work through the finer points of *how* to get there. He helps the prospect see who and what else may be needed to make the overall solution a success.

V.

THE MODERN SELLER IS AN **AMBASSADOR**

CHAPTER 13

Strategies to Build Modern Ambassadors

Account plans. Territory plans. Vertical plans. Quarterly business reviews. These are the usual activities we do and documents we create in our sales organizations—all with the intention of growing our books of business. But most of those files start collecting digital dust the moment we finish them.

What if we took a different approach to the usual account planning? What if we took the approach of being an ambassador, one that also creates ambassadors out of our prospects and clients? That dual approach would set us apart—as individual sellers, sales leaders, and organizations.

The Ambassador Profile contains a set of inventories to help you do that. You can use these inventories to evaluate and increase the lifetime value in your most important accounts, territories, or verticals. These inventories can also help you evaluate competitive segments you want to break into. The higher the lifetime value, the lower your risk for losing hard-won prospects and clients to a competitor. And the greater your odds of success in reaching your biggest sales goals.

The Ambassador Profile directly ties to the other elements of modern selling. For example, your Ambassador Profile might include:

- Your vision and territory strategies from the **Entrepreneurial** dimension.
- Processes for your sales and your customer buying cycles from the **Holistic** dimension.
- The network ecosystems you mapped out in the **Social** dimension.
- The skill development areas you identified in the **Agile** dimension.

Ambassador Profile Inventories

There are four key inventories for your Ambassador Profile. Each play a role in how you create and receive overall value. Depending on the client or selling situation you're working with, choose the inventories which are the best fit for you.

- Lifetime Value Inventory
- Loyalty Engagement Inventory
- Key Relationships Inventory
- Brand Profile Inventory

Strategy No. 1: Understand a Client's Lifetime Value

Ambassadors believe the initial win is only the first step in creating lifetime value. They know lifetime value goes both ways, and it's a mutual partnership. Value is created *by you* for the prospect or client. Over time, that value should also be created *for you*, as an individual and as a company. Every activity has the possibility of either adding to or subtracting from the overall lifetime value of the relationship.

The Lifetime Value Inventory provides a snapshot of where you are today on the value continuum, and guides you on what else is needed to establish and grow that value. This profile is ideal for RFP situations because it can help you make go or no-go decisions on pursuing an RFP.

Maybe most importantly, it can tell you if you're trying to create lifetime value and there's a fundamental mismatch.

This reminds me of a past client—a large, urban school district. This school district, like many, would put out an intensive bid process every time they needed to make a technology purchase. They were required to do so because of their funding model—they received significant public funds from governments and agencies.

As hard as I tried to use modern selling approaches, I was never able to break out of the vendor box. It was always about price.

After lots of losing, frustration, and some digging, I figured out more behind their why. Most, if not all, of the students in this district relied on the school for so much more than just learning. It was a safety net. They were fed two hot meals a day, and received a structured after-school environment. These kids weren't fortunate enough to get those basics at home, so in many ways, school became their home.

Then it clicked for me.

I realized their top lifetime value criterion was initial price.

Because every dollar they immediately saved in one budget area (like buying my technology) was a dollar that could go to meals, books, and after-school programs. The reality was that my biggest competitor was the best fit for them. My competitor aligned with their key lifetime value criterion—products at a lower initial price point and good enough for the need. That experience taught me that lifetime value must match in order to create long-term success. I also learned there are times when our clients' priorities are more significant than what we sell.

How to use the Lifetime Value Inventory

Below are some lifetime value criteria to consider as you're creating your inventory. Each one provides data for a more complete view into whether your prospect, client, or selling situation has enough potential lifetime value to invest your time, effort, and resources.

You'll want to rate yourself two ways: First, your perspective of where this prospect, client, or selling situation rates today in creating lifetime value for you. Second, your honest look of how your prospect or client views you/your company and the lifetime value you create for them.

As you rate each item, some may apply more to you as the seller, and some may apply more to the buyer's viewpoint.

Use a rating scale of 1 to 10, with 10 being the highest indicator of lifetime value, and 1 being the lowest. If you use all the criteria, the highest total for each column is 120 points, and a total value of 240 points.

CATEGORY	How would you/ your company rate the prospect or client?	How would your prospect or client rate you/your company?
Philosophical Alignment – Rates how well your overall values, vision, and business philosophies align.		
Sales Process – Rates the ease of doing business and clarity during the sales process; access to the right leadership levels for decision making; transparency of information sharing.		
Solution Compatibility – How well your solution portfolio aligns to their functional or technical requirements.		
Post-sales Onboarding – Rates the experience after the deal is won. There's a clear, simple, and effective process reinforcing that the client made the right decision to do business with you.		

CATEGORY	How would you/ your company rate the prospect or client?	How would your prospect or client rate you/your company?
Internal Team Support – The right teams are in place to support the client post-onboarding. There are clear and simple support processes, and specific points of contact to guide the client.		
Price/Fee Sensitivity – Rates how likely this prospect or client is to accept your prices or fees, or if they will tend to significantly negotiate. This is both a short-term and long-term view.		
Revenue – Rates revenue potential, short-term and long-term. Consider overall scale of revenue potential as well.		
Profitability – Rates the overall profit potential, both short-term and long-term. How important is the profitability of this client to you?		
Administration – Rates daily operations. For example, products and services delivered on time; the client pays their invoices in a timely manner.		
Growth/Cross-Sell Potential – Rates growth potential, and the ability to cross-sell new products/services within the client once the initial deal is won.		
Referenceability – Rates how referenceable this client will be; for example, they are open to creating a case study for success, or they are willing to provide testimonials on your behalf.		
Logo Strength – Rates how important this prospect or client is to your portfolio of logos. For example, this company may be a cornerstone client or help you gain credibility in a new market.		

Using 240 points, this scale will help you interpret the data.

0-80 Points: Low odds of meaningful lifetime value. Unless there's a key category heavily outweighing the others, this prospect or client isn't worth your investment. This score can also indicate the need for more information to make an informed decision.

81-160 Points: Mid-range odds of lifetime value, and worth considering the investment. Look for any patterns that indicate where you may need to invest. Also look for large swings between your perspective and a prospect/client's perspective. That could indicate a deeper challenge to overcome, or perhaps the need for more information. This is the widest ranging tier; one thing to keep in mind is that a prospect or client that scores 90 is likely very different from one that scores 150.

161-240 Points: High odds of lifetime value, and worth the investment! You'll want to look for ways to continue adding (and receiving) lifetime value, to keep the overall score at these high levels.

Strategy No. 2: Create 29 Percenters

The second inventory for your Ambassador Profile is about loyalty engagement. As you think about your existing customers and clients, how many of them can you say are actively engaged with you and with your company's brand? How many of them would never switch to a competitor?

Research from Gallup indicates that only 29 percent of clients are truly engaged with us; the other 71 percent fall somewhere else on the satisfaction spectrum. This could mean that they range anywhere from very satisfied all the way to completely disengaged, and maybe looking for that next opportunity to switch.

You want 29 percenters.

An example from my own life is that I fly frequently for work. Even if another airline offers a lower fare or a direct flight, Southwest Airlines is always the first airline I choose.

Why?

Because they've earned not just satisfaction with me, but over time that satisfaction has turned into loyalty. The evolution into loyalty has happened for two core reasons. First, they deliver consistently on table stakes. Getting me and my luggage safely and on time to my destination are the table stakes. Second, there's an emotional connection to my experience. I feel stress free (as stress-free as you get in airports anyway). I have a sense of freedom because I can easily change my travel plans. And, I feel welcomed every time I travel with Southwest.

I specifically remember one time I was traveling to Dallas on business, and there was a rare snow storm. This was one time where I happened to be flying another airline. You know that feeling when you see every flight, one after another, showing "cancelled" on the departure screen? I was going to be stuck for two additional days, unless I figured out another plan.

I figured every airline would be having these problems but decided to check Southwest anyway. I called the 1-800 number (old school) and actually got a real, live person within the first few minutes of my call. I call this table stakes, but with a little extra, given how hard it can be to reach a live person.

There was one flight left for the day getting back to Columbus, connecting in Orlando (no snow!). This agent immediately booked me on that flight for no charge, and because it was leaving so soon, made the extra effort to be sure that the gate agent knew I would be coming. I was so relieved and happy to make it home that day. That experience made me a loyal 29 percenter.

The difference between table stakes satisfaction and loyalty is emotional connection. It's the bridge where engagement happens, where those 29 percenters are. And the more clients you have that are like those 29 percenters, the more you can build lifetime value.

Building loyalty is a process. It's not something that happens all at once, but it's built over time in stages. An article in the *Austin Business Journal* by author Jill Griffin describes this process as the evolution of starting as a prospect, to becoming a first-time customer, to becoming a repeat and regular customer, and finally becoming a raving fan and advocate. Each stage in the journey solidifies the relationship more, to the point where that client can't imagine buying your product or service from anyone else.

To create your Loyalty Engagement Inventory, you'll first want to determine where you are today. Where does your client fall on the loyalty spectrum, or what is your prospect's potential for loyalty? With that information, you can design and implement the right strategies to help you build and maintain loyalty.

How to Use the Loyalty Engagement Inventory

Each of the loyalty categories are traits or outcomes you want to have in your current clients and build in your prospects over time, once they become clients. As you read the following statements in each category, how would you rate yourself?

On this scale, 1 means the loyalty factor is extremely low, and 5 means the loyalty factor is extremely high.

If you're evaluating a prospect and don't have enough information, this tool can be used to work with them, so you better understand what would make them raving fans and advocates.

CATEGORY	STATEMENT	RATING (1-5)
TRUSTED ADVISOR: I have trusted advisor status with this current client. If this is a prospect, I am firmly establishing myself as a trusted advisor.	I proactively provide value, in the form of expertise, connections, or other resources.	
	This prospect/client consults with me early when issues arise. They don't wait until it's an even bigger issue.	
	This prospect/client turns to me for guidance within my area of expertise.	
	This prospect/client turns to me for guidance outside of my area of expertise, because they know I can connect them to the right resources.	
	I am continually learning and curious on a wide range of topics, so I can share that learning with this prospect or client.	
CREATING ADVOCATES: This client is actively engaged and advocates on my behalf. The relationship has helped me to exponentially grow my book of business.	This client actively refers business to me.	
	This client provides testimonials for me and willingly talks about their experience to my prospects when I make the request.	
	This client actively seeks out ways for us to continue doing business together.	
	This client willingly uses their own social capital to open doors for me.	
	If my advocate at this client left their current employer, they would bring me into their next employer.	

CATEGORY	STATEMENT	RATING (1-5)
OVERALL EXPERIENCE: This prospect/client buys on value, they don't default to price.	This prospect/client is a value-based buyer. They place significant business value on my product or service.	
	This prospect/client doesn't typically try to negotiate down on price.	
	Our delivery experience after the sale is consistently strong.	
	I have a deep understanding of what my prospect or client values. That understanding is documented, and I review it regularly with my client.	
	I have created ways for my customers to provide feedback beyond my company processes. I regularly monitor and respond to that feedback.	
	How I deliver the product, service, or experience differentiates me from my competitor.	
GETTING TO YES: This prospect/client sees us on the "same side of the table." They always look for ways to create a Yes situation.	I've successfully recovered from a past issue at this client.	
	The client will proactively tell me when something isn't working. They'll give me a true chance to resolve it, or we'll resolve it together.	
	I can openly tell the client when something isn't working. I'll give them a true chance to resolve it, or we'll resolve it together.	
	There's a high level of accountability in our relationship, and a very low level of blame.	

Using 100 points, this scale will help you interpret the data.

0-40 Points: Your loyalty factor is low and could indicate a disengaged client. This is an opportunity to determine what level of investment you feel is worth making to improve the relationship. This score can also indicate the need for more information, or you could be in the beginning stages of the relationship and need more time.

41-75 Points: You likely have a satisfied but not fully engaged client. Look for any patterns to direct you on where to invest in improving loyalty. This is the widest ranging tier, so one thing to keep in mind is that the engagement level of a client with a score of 45 is likely very different from one that scores 75.

76-100 Points: You likely have a highly engaged client, a "29 percenter." This is likely a cornerstone or flagship client, and one that's worth the continued investment. Take what you're learning from this client and apply it to other clients where you'd like to increase loyalty.

Strategy No. 3: Amplify Your Key Relationships

The connected economy, the Amazon effect, and the commoditization tipping point I mentioned earlier are at work in our relationships, whether it's a long-time client or brand new prospect.

Here's how those three factors recently played out for me. As someone who's just a shade over five feet all, I love to wear heels. In practically any business setting, you're going to see in me in heels. But after about two or three hours, I'm dying for my running shoes. I carry a pair of flats with me wherever I go for a quick and pain-free getaway.

There's a podcast I tune into very regularly, *Glambition Radio* from entrepreneur Ali Brown. I've followed Ali for years as a trusted resource, and highly recommend her podcast to women in business. She's always finding interesting guests I wouldn't normally come across. During one day of drive time, I was listening as she interviewed the CEO of a company called Vivian Lou. It was a company I'd never heard of until then. As it turned out, Vivian Lou was an exclusive global distributor of shoe inserts designed specifically for women who didn't want to give up their heels but can't take the foot pain any longer.

It's probably completely predictable what I did when I got home.

I jump on both Amazon and Vivian Lou websites at the same time to compare products, reviews, and recommendations. I've become a prospective buyer, now connected to this unknown company by a trusted resource. The Amazon effect has kicked in. I see hundreds of four and five-star reviews. While I don't personally know any of these reviewers, we have our shoe challenge in common and this product solved that challenge for them. So, I determined, it could work for me, too.

I decide to buy a two-pack of the couture brand of inserts, which is their most effective and expensive insert. This high-end option is only available on the Vivian Lou website (resisting the commoditization tipping point). But very smartly, I'm offered free two-day shipping on my order. The last comparison barrier, over what amounts to $5 worth of shipping, has been removed. Because I've purchased directly through their website I'm now on their mailing list; they can communicate with me, learn more about me, and increase the potential for overall lifetime value.

I bet you have a similar story (maybe minus the heels).

Taking a step back, if we dissect our patterns, many of our consumer buying habits are rooted in trusted relationships, social proof, and relevance. We bring these same habits to our business buying patterns. Some Nielsen research backs that up. We're more than four times likely to buy when referred by a friend or trusted resource. In fact, 92 percent of us will trust referrals from people we know or have a shared challenge in common.

If you've worked through the Social dimension of modern selling, you already have your significant goals and a map of your network ecosystem. With the Key Relationships Inventory, we'll also expand it to include things like testimonials, referrals, and strategic alliances.

How to Use the Key Relationships Inventory

The categories below represent the types of relationships you want to build in your current clients and evaluate in your prospective ones. It's also a snapshot of your broader relationships outside of your customer base. As you read the following statements in each category, how would you rate yourself?

On this scale, 1 means the key relationship factor is extremely low right now, and 5 means the key relationship factor is extremely high.

If you're evaluating a prospect and don't have enough information, use this tool to help you evaluate their potential, or identify your priorities and goals once they've become a client.

CATEGORY	STATEMENT	RATING (1-5)
REFERRALS: Strategic introductions and opportunity creation within my networks.	My client actively makes referral introductions for me inside of his/her organization.	
	My client actively makes referral introductions for me outside of his/her organization.	
	I have an identified and active peer referral network; we specifically make introductions and create opportunities for one another.	
	I have an effective process for requesting referrals from clients.	
TESTIMONIALS: Current and results-oriented documentation of the value I bring to my clients.	I have a collection of testimonials or use cases I can easily access and share with prospective clients. Where appropriate, they're viewable in my professional/social profiles.	
	My testimonials or use cases are results-oriented and current.	
	I can easily think of three clients who would enthusiastically take a phone call from my prospect; they would talk highly about the value of my work and the relationship.	
	I have an effective process for requesting testimonials from clients.	
CENTERS OF INFLUENCE: Individuals or organizations that open doors, provide insights, and create environments to build strategic relationships.	I have access to the centers of influence relevant to this prospect or client.	
	I am on a high-profile committee or I'm an active contributor to a high-profile organization – one that routinely involves centers of influence.	
	I regularly get requests from others for my insights, ideas, and connections related to my area of expertise.	
	I routinely make connections for others in my network; I connect them to people, resources, and ideas that are relevant to them.	

CATEGORY	STATEMENT	RATING (1-5)
BUYING ROLES: Within a specific selling situation, these are the individuals involved in influencing the decision-making process.	I have a current map of the buying roles in my prospect or client selling situation. I know the power structure and where the influence lies.	
	I am actively cultivating relationships at all levels of the buying structure.	
	I have at least two advocates within the prospect or client who provide me with insights to the buying structure.	
	I know who my final decision maker is, and I have access to that person (even if the decision-making process involves a committee).	
STRATEGIC ALLIANCES: Partnerships that create complimentary opportunities; they're often revenue-generating and provide value I wouldn't otherwise be able to provide.	I understand the challenges and aspirations within my prospect or client, beyond just what my product or service can solve for them.	
	I have and actively leverage alliances (formal or informal) with providers that are complimentary to what my company provides.	
	These strategic alliances are financially beneficial; they generate revenue, profit, and commissions for all partners.	
	These strategic alliances help me to be more valuable to my clients and give me a competitive advantage.	

Using 100 points, this scale will help you interpret the data.

0-40 Points: Your key relationship factors are low; this is likely negatively impacting your effectiveness as a modern seller. While your scoring may be prospect or client specific, you'll want to take a bigger picture view of your overall approach to key relationships. In any categories where you scored yourself a 1 or 2, select one of those as your starting point. When you make improvements in one area, it will begin to positively affect other areas.

41-75 Points: You're solidly within the mid-tier. Look for categories where you're currently strong and continue to amplify those. Add to the mix by choosing a category that's out of your comfort zone and focus your efforts there.

76-100 Points: Your approach to key relationships are the definition of modern selling. Continue to amplify your areas of strength. To keep yourself on track, focus on any questions where you scored yourself a 3 or lower.

Strategy No. 4: Become a Brand Standout

In my own evolution from professional seller to entrepreneur, an important shift occurred. I was stepping into a brighter personal spotlight and my brand became much more visible. As I was growing my book of business on my own name and reputation, it became clearer to me that my clients were buying me and not the logo on my business card. They knew my name first, my company name second.

One customer situation really drove this home for me.

I was bidding on a large opportunity and made it to the final round. The top three solution providers would present to the key decision maker and her team. It was an RFP situation, and would be consensus by committee before it made its final stop at the decision maker's desk. (I'm pretty sure there were at least 6.8 people on their committee, just like CEB's research would show.) The competitors were well-known companies, with high brand recognition and lots of resources to throw at a presentation. They would add at least another 6.8 people to the room to show how well-resourced they were.

Because my company brand recognition would be low in comparison, I made it my mission to be a unique personal standout. I made it my mission that they would equate me, and then my team, and then my company brand, with their success. This meant doing things like:

- Requesting individual discovery calls with each committee member and members of the procurement team.
- Creating a highly customized presentation about them (not about me or my company) that hit on the hot button points.
- Taking a reverse approach to the presentation optics, by purposely bringing a small team. They would sit among the prospect's team and not across a big conference room table, so the prospect could envision us working together.
- Planning a creative implementation approach that would save the client hundreds of thousands of dollars in fees.
- Committing to donate a portion of the profits to a non-profit of their choice.
- Handwritten notes to every committee member.

These were the details I could control. They went beyond the usual presentation conversations around things like pricing and technical excellence. They made an impression about the overall experience that my competitors didn't match. Each detail created an ambassador experience. We went on to win that initial deal, and also the opportunity to build future lifetime value.

Ambassadors are unique standouts when it comes to brand. They can blend their personal brand and their company's brand in a way that supports their individuality but also reinforces the reputation of their company.

Ambassadors also know that part of a strong brand isn't about what they sell, it's about how they sell it, and the experience they provide. The how and the experience are unique to them and can't be commoditized. They believe that what the customer is really buying into is them. An excellent product or service backed by a reputable team and company are table stakes. The company's brand reputation is important, but it almost becomes secondary. That's where building a Brand Profile Inventory comes in.

How to Use the Brand Profile Inventory

The Brand Profile Inventory will help you to assess yourself against the key brand attributes of an ambassador. As you read the following statements, how would you rate yourself?

One this scale, 1 means the ambassador brand factor is extremely low right now, and 5 means the brand factor is extremely high.

AMBASSADOR BRAND FACTOR	RATING (1-5)
Owner: I take ownership for all facets of the prospect or client relationship. I'm the face of the relationship in their eyes.	
Expert: I am actively developing my expertise in three areas: my industry, my sales craft, and one personal passion.	
Elevator: I'm known for leaving a situation better than I found it. I'm known for creating positive forward movement and lift.	
Impact Oriented: I selectively challenge the status quo, when it will create positive impact or avoid negative impact.	
Strategic and Tactical: I routinely have business-level conversations (the what) and pivot to technical or functional conversations (the how).	
Unifier: I am known for finding commonalities and mutual benefit, especially in conflict situations.	
Loyalty Magnet: At least 50 percent of my book of business is repeat business.	
Lifetime Value Creator: I would rather "win for a lifetime" over "win for right now."	

AMBASSADOR BRAND FACTOR	RATING (1-5)
Thought Leader: I regularly publish original thought leadership and also share the thought leadership of other trusted subject matter experts with my network.	
Brand Standout: I'm highly recognized as a leader in my industry, within my organization, and within my territory.	

Using 50 points, this scale will help you interpret the data.

0-21 Points: Your ambassador brand factors are low; this will negatively impact your long-term effectiveness as a modern seller. In any areas where you scored yourself a 1 or 2, select one of those as your starting point. When you make improvements in one area, it will begin to positively affect other areas.

22-40 Points: You're solidly within the mid-tier. Continue to amplify the categories where you're currently strong. Add to the mix by choosing a category that's out of your comfort zone and focus your efforts there.

41-50 Points: Your ambassador brand factors are high, and the definition of modern selling! Continue to amplify those high scoring areas. If there are any categories where you scored below a 3, that can become a focus area to keep you on track.

KEY TAKEAWAYS

- Ambassadors are a bridge, connecting themselves and their organization to prospects, customers, the greater community, and relevant industries.
- As unique standouts, ambassadors blend their individual brand with that of their organization. This creates value for them as individuals, for their organization, and for their customers.
- For an ambassador, initial wins are important, but creating lifetime value is even more important.
- The ambassador dimension of modern selling matters for four key reasons: we're evolving toward an economy where relationships are our most valuable currency; creating satisfaction is no longer enough in today's sales economy; the Amazon effect has reached B2B selling; even the most sophisticated products and services are being commoditized.
- Today's sales economy requires a different approach to the usual account and territory planning. The Ambassador Profile is designed to do that, with four key inventories: lifetime value, loyalty engagement, key relationships, and brand profile. It's an approach that will give you a competitive advantage.

VI.

EPILOGUE

Putting It All Together

The new sales economy is here to stay, and with it will come continual, rapid change and big challenges. The business, technology, and cultural dynamics that create it will always be evolving. But the new sales economy is also full of opportunity. Modern sellers and leaders will be the ones who turn those opportunities into successes.

When I set out to write this book, I wanted to dig into the "skills behind the skills" that would make the biggest difference for you, my reader, on your path to modern selling.

Here's what I uncovered: First, skills are only one part of the modern selling equation. Equally important are your mindset, your tools, your processes, and the people with whom you surround yourself. It's why I ultimately landed on calling these dimensions.

Second, these dimensions don't necessarily replace your everyday sales activities. Instead, they amplify your most high-value sales activities, so you can be more efficient, more effective, and have greater impact. You will sell more in the new sales economy.

Living the Modern Seller Definition

The modern seller definition is really for any sales or leadership situation. Consider it a guidepost for all of your interactions. I like to think of it as a way of both being and operating in our connected sales world. To revisit our definition of a modern seller:

> ***A modern seller is one who's recognized as a differentiator in their customer's business, and the value of their product or service isn't fully recognized without them. A modern seller's customer sees their work, done together, as strategic to their competitive advantage.***

Below are a few questions to help keep the definition top of mind:

- Am I being a differentiator today?
- Am I extending the value of my product or service?
- Am I someone who my prospects, customers, partners, and my organization see as invaluable to their success?

Where to from here?

This book may be the starting point of your work on the 5 Dimensions of a Modern Seller, but you'll continue to hone them throughout your sales career and beyond. I like to think of the 5 Dimensions as habits. And like habits, they take time, commitment, and patience to build. But the great thing about the building process is that you don't have to wait to reap the benefits. You'll benefit while you build them.

Here are a few other parting thoughts:

Start with the dimension that's the best fit for you. There's no best place to start, just as long as you start. And keep going.

Habits beget habits. Don't be surprised if, for example, you're working on the Agile dimension and see a positive ripple effect in the other dimensions—as well as your sales results.

Make it a collaborative effort. Partner with colleagues or your leaders. Get an accountability partner. Challenge each another to make these dimensions part of your daily conversations. If you're a leader, the exercises can be built into your coaching activities, your sales meetings, or other team sales routines.

Modern sellers are leaders. This book is about leadership as much as it is about sales. When you, the modern seller, are agile, entrepreneurial, holistic, social, and an ambassador, you're also a leader. Leadership is a daily (and sometimes moment-by-moment) choice. When you're building these modern skills, you're also choosing to be a leader.

I wish you continued success, and I'm looking forward to continuing the modern selling journey with you.

NOTES AND CITATIONS

Author's Note

1. Gerhard Gschwandtner. The Digital Transformation to Sales 3.0. Presented at the Sales 3.0 Conference, September 2017.
2. Bonchek, Mark. "How to Create an Exponential Mindset." *Harvard Business Review*. July 27, 2016: https://hbr.org/2016/07/how-to-create-an-exponential-mindset

Introduction

1. The Radicati Group, Inc. Email Statistics Report, 2014 – 2018. (http://www.radicati.com/wp/wp-content/uploads/2014/01/Email-Statistics-Report-2014-2018-Executive-Summary.pdf)
2. Morin, Amy. "Waiting for a Reply? Study Explains the Psychology Behind Email Response Time." (https://www.forbes.com/sites/amymorin/2015/11/28/waiting-for-a-reply-study-explains-the-psychology-behind-email-response-time/#6347171b9755
3. Kotter, John. "Change Fatigue: Taking Its Toll on Your Employees?" https://www.forbes.com/sites/johnkotter/2011/09/15/can-i-use-this-method-for-change-in-my-organization/#6a82c6941ce6
4. Employee Tenure in 2016. Bureau of Labor Statistics News Release. https://www.bls.gov/news.release/pdf/tenure.pdf
5. Guide to Customer Centricity: Analytics and Advice for B2B Leaders. Gallup, Inc. 2016. www.gallup.com/file/services/188879/B2BGuide_Reports_201602.pdf
6. Lerner, Jennifer S., et al. "Emotion and Decision Making." https://scholar. harvard.edu/files/jenniferlerner/files/annual_review_manuscript_june_16_final.final_.pdf; page 7.

Make Way for the Modern Seller

1. Holmes, Julie. CEO, Inline Strategy. https://www.linkedin.com/in/thejulieholmes/

Agile

1. Expanding the Leadership Equation: Developing Next Generation Leaders. Whitepaper: Issued October 2012, reprinted September 2015. The Center for Creative Leadership. http://www.ccl.org/wp-content/uploads/2015/04/ExpandingLeadershipEquation.pdf
2. The #1 factor of high performing organizations. Association for Talent Development, 2016 International Conference. Author's notes from keynote by CEO Tony Bingham. May 23, 2016.
3. Valcour, Monique. "4 Ways to Become a Better Learner." *Harvard Business* Review. https://hbr.org/2015/12/4-ways-to-become-a-better-learner
4. Flaum, J.P., and Betty Winkler. "Improve Your Ability to Learn." *Harvard Business Review.* https://hbr.org/2015/06/improve-your-ability-to-learn
5. Cashman, Kevin. "The Five Dimensions of Learning Agile Leaders." *Forbes* https://www.forbes.com/sites/kevincashman/2013/04/03/ the-five-dimensions-of-learning-agile-leaders/#39169fca7457
6. Guide to Customer Centricity: Analytics and Advice for B2B Leaders. Gallup, Inc. 2016. Page 30. www.gallup.com/file/services/188879/B2BGuide_Reports_201602.pdf
7. DeMeuse, Kenneth P. "What's Smarter than I.Q.?" Korn Ferry Institute. March 2017. http://leadershipall.com/wp-content/uploads/2012/12/Whats-smarter-than-IQ.pdf
8. "Brain Fills Gaps to Produce Likely Picture." Radboud University Nijmegen, June 27, 2014. https://www.sciencedaily.com/releases/2014/06/140627094551.htm
9. Ramachandran, Vilayanur S. and Diane Rogers-Ramachandran. "Mind the Gap." Scientific American. April 2005. https:// www.scientificamerican.com/article/mind-the-gap/
10. Atkinson, Tom and Steve Barry. "Learning at Top Speed." Chief Learning Officer, January 2010.
11. Coleman, John. "The Best Strategic Leaders Balance Agility and Consistency." *Harvard Business Review*, January 2017. https://hbr. org/2017/01/the-best-strategic-leaders-balance-agility-and-consistency

12. David, Susan. "Building Emotional Agility." *Harvard Business Review*, September 22, 2017. HBR IdeaCast. https://hbr.org/ideacast/2016/09/building-emotional-agility
13. Duhigg, Charles. *The Power of Habit: Why We Do What We Do in Life and Business*. Pages 19-20. Duhigg's citation for Ann M. Graybiel: "Neurotransmitters and Neuromodulators in the Basal Ganglia," Trends in Neurosciences 13 (1990): 244-54.
14. Robinett, Judy. *How to be a Power Connector: The 5+50+100 Rule for Turning Your Business Network into Profits.*
15. Franko, Amy, Jen E. Miller, and Brittany Shonka. 6 Strategies to Maximize Sales Results. https://amyfranko.com/resources/ebooks/6-strategies-maximize-sales-results/
16. Martin, Steve W. University of Southern California Marshall School of Business. Heavy Hitters Sales Blog: http://heavyhittersales.typepad.com/; http://blog. thecenterforsalesstrategy.com/personality-traits-of-top-sales-performers
17. Southwest Magazine, October 2016 issue; page 47. https://issuu.com/southwestmag/docs/oct2016/47

Entrepreneurial

1. Deutsch, Waverly, and Craig Wortmann. Entrepreneurial Selling. Polsky Center for Entrepreneurship, University of Chicago Booth School of Business.
2. Research firm Forrester describes it as a "variety of touchpoints by which the customer moves from awareness to engagement and purchase." Forrester Research on customer journey. https://www.forrester.com/Customer-Journey
3. Wexner's approach is that the time to change things is when they aren't broken. The time to change is before commoditization sets in or disruption is so far along that you're finding yourself with a lot of catching up to do to stay relevant. https://impactinstruction.com/leadership/6-tips-for-being-a-better-leader-from-successful-ceos/

4. Westwood, Ryan. "The Traits Entrepreneurs Need to Succeed." *Forbes*, January 9, 2017. https://www.forbes.com/sites/ryanwestwood/2017/01/09/the-traits-entrepreneurs-need-to-succeed
5. Lee, Hau L. "Don't Tweak Your Supply Chain — Rethink It End to End." *Harvard Business Review*, October 2010. https://hbr.org/2010/10/dont-tweak-your-supply-chain-rethink-it-end-to-end
6. Brosseau, Denise. *Ready to be a Thought Leader?* Jossey- Bass, 2013. http://www.thoughtleadershiplab.com/Resources/WhatIsaThoughtLeader
7. "Targeting," "finding small and specific markets." Deutsch, Waverly, and Craig Wortmann. Entrepreneurial Selling. Polsky Center for Entrepreneurship, University of Chicago Booth School of Business. Pages 10-14.
8. Rasmus, Daniel. "The Golden Rules for Creating Thoughtful Thought Leadership." *Fast Company*, December 12, 2012. https://www.fastcompany.com/3003897/golden-rules-creating-thoughtful-thought-leadership

Holistic

1. Hewlett, Sylvia Ann, et al. Executive Presence: http://www.talentinnovation.org/assets/ExecutivePresence-KeyFindings-CTI.pdf
2. Hewlett, Sylvia Ann. *Executive Presence: The Missing Link Between Merit and Success.*
3. Hewlett, Sylvia Ann. "Executive Presence: Talks at Google." https://www.youtube.com/watch?v=i2QOAfWLedE
4. Gelles, David. "At Aetna, a CEO's Management by Matra." *New York Times*: February 27, 2015. https://www.nytimes.com/2015/03/01/business/at-aetna-a-ceos-management-by-mantra.html
5. Kruse, Kevin. *15 Secrets Successful People Know About Time Management.* The Kruse Group, 2015. Pages 16-18. www.kevinkruse.com
6. Duhigg, Charles. *Smarter Faster Better: The Secrets of Being Productive in Life and Business.* Page 243.

7. Women for Economic and Leadership Development. Leadership session with Angel investor John Huston, who introduced me to the concept of being versus doing. From the author's personal notes, circa 2008-2009.
8. Keller, Gary and Jay Papasan. *The One Thing: The Surprisingly Simple Truth Behind Extraordinary Results.* Page 106.
9. Konrath, Jill. *Selling to Big Companies.*
10. "Why You Should Write a Failure Resume." Dr. Tina Seelig and Dan Pink. http://www.danpink.com/pinkcast/pinkcast-1-12-why-you- should-write-a-failure-resume/
11. Valcour, Monique. "Beating Burnout." *Harvard Business Review.* November 2016. https://hbr.org/2016/11/beating-burnout
12. Ferriss, Timothy. *The 4-Hour Workweek: Escape 9-5, Live Anywhere, and Join the New Rich.* Pages 45-47.
13. Atkinson, Jane. The Wealthy Speaker: www.wealthyspeaker.com and www.speakerlauncher.com.

Social

1. Leading B2B Sales Organizations Challenge, Align & Prescribe To Get Deals Done. CEB. https://news.cebglobal.com/2016-11-21-Leading- B2B-Sales-Organizations-Challenge-Align-Prescribe-To-Get-Deals- Done]
2. Robinett, Judy. *How to Be a Power Connector: The 5 + 50 + 100 Rule for Turning Your Business Network into Profits.* Pages 59-67.
3. Dweck, Carol. "Mindset: The New Psychology of Success." https://mindsetonline.com/
4. Ferrazzi, Keith. Generosity Breeds Connection. Work/Life Integration Project. http://worklife.wharton.upenn.edu/2014/09/generosity- breeds-connection-keith-ferrazzi/
5. Ibarra Herminia, and Mark Lee Hunter. "How Leaders Create and Use Networks." *Harvard Business Review.* January 2007: https://hbr.org/2007/01/how-leaders-create-and-use-networks

Ambassador

1. Corporate culture expert Greg Hawks. www.hawksagency.com
2. Atkinson, Tom and Steve Barry. "Learning at Top Speed." Chief Learning Officer, January 2010. Page 27.
3. Annex Cloud Blog. https://www.annexcloud.com/blog/2016/11/23/b2b-loyalty-statistics-take-advantage-of-an-overlooked-opportunity/
   a. Griffin, Jill. Customer Loyalty. http://altfeldinc.com/pdfs/Customer%20Loyalty.pdf
6. SAS Insights blog. https://www.sas.com/en_us/insights/articles/marketing/seth-godins-rules-for-marketing-in-the-new-economy.html#
7. Fortune 500 Archives. http://archive.fortune.com/magazines/fortune/fortune500_archive/full/1955/
8. Rain Group. "How Clients Buy: 2009 Benchmark Report on Professional Services Marketing & Selling from the Client Perspective." Page 15.
9. Annex Cloud Blog: https://www.annexcloud.com/blog/2016/11/23/b2b-loyalty-statistics-take-advantage-of-an-overlooked-opportunity/
   a. "Often Overlooked in M&A: Customers and Employees." http://news.gallup.com/businessjournal/186875/often-overlooked-customers-employees.aspx
10. Griffin, Jill. "Keep Your Customer Loyal, Not Just Satisfied." Austin Business Journal. January 17, 1999. https://www.bizjournals.com/austin/stories/1999/01/18/smallb3.html
11. Brown, Ali. Glambition Radio. Episode 132, featuring Abby Lou Walker. https://itunes.apple.com/us/podcast/glambition-radio/id799805829
12. Annex Cloud Blog: https://www.annexcloud.com/blog/2016/03/03/39-referral-marketing-statistics-that-will-make-you-want-to-start-a-raf-program-tomorrow/
    a. Under the Influence: Consumer Trust in Advertising: http://www.nielsen.com/us/en/insights/news/2013/under-the-influence-consumer-trust-in-advertising.html

ACKNOWLEDGEMENTS

This book is something I've held as a longtime dream and goal, and it took nearly two years to make it a reality. With any significant goal, it's never done alone, and I'm definitely no exception. There are dozens of people who have played a role, big and small.

I'd like to take a moment here to thank you. Thank you for the valuable feedback, the words of encouragement, and the genuine support along the way. A few specifically I'd like to mention:

My husband, Dave Franko. From the day I jumped into entrepreneurship, you've always been my biggest supporter, cheerleader, and source of logic. We're in it together, and I'm so grateful.

My fellow entrepreneurs. We all know this can feel like a solitary road at times, and I've been fortunate to have entrepreneur friends across the globe to share in the struggles and successes. To the Columbus, Ohio community especially, your entrepreneurial spirit and openness are unmatched.

My friends and family. While you may not really know what I do for a living or where I'm going most of the time, you always ask how it's going and what you can do to support me.

My clients. I get to work with the best and I appreciate your trust.

My team. You keep the wheels on the bus moving. I'm grateful for your expertise, your can-do spirit, and the opportunity to work alongside you.

My new friends at Smart Business. To a person, they've all been as invested in the success of this book as I have. They've paid attention to every detail and I couldn't have picked a better publishing partner.